P9-APX-960

WATER FLYING

Cessna 150 on Edo floats. Many youngsters celebrate their 16th birthday by making their first legal solo flight. (Edo Aircraft)

WATER FLYING

Franklin T. Kurt

INTRODUCTION BY
Wolfgang Langewiesche

MACMILLAN PUBLISHING CO., INC.
New York

COLLIER MACMILLAN PUBLISHERS
London

This book is dedicated to the reader.

May it widen your horizons,
improve your judgment and skill,
expand the usefulness of your airplane
and lead to more flying fun than you've ever known!

Library of Congress Cataloging in Publication Data
Kurt, Franklin T
Water flying.
1. Seaplanes. 2. Seaplanes—Piloting. I. Title.
TL684.K87 629.133'347 73-13362
ISBN 0-02-567130-8

Macmillan Publishing Co., Inc.
866 Third Avenue, New York, N.Y. 10022
Collier-Macmillan Canada Ltd.

First Printing 1974

Printed in the United States of America

CONTENTS

ACKNOWLEDGMENTS

This book is far from a one-man effort. Many old web-footed pilot friends have contributed. New friendships were made. Among them are the true Collaborators to whom I now express my deepest appreciation.

James C. Reddig. A life-long friend and designer of the superb Fleet Wings Sea Bird Amphibian.

Erik Hofman. Of Mallorca, another life-long friend who ascertained that I made no omissions.

Grover Loening. The honored dean of all American aviation and the master seaplane designer, who rightfully prefers the name "waterplanes" to "seaplanes."

David B. Thurston. A friend of many years who is now the leading flying boat designer, Dave could easily have written all of Part Two himself.

Leighton Collins. He launched this book and his analysis and comments in *Air Facts* have guided all phases of general aviation for four decades.

Percival H. Spencer. Designer, home builder and seaplane pilot since 1914—and still at it.

John Batchelor. Of Broadhurst, England, he selected and donated the photographs of the outstanding European flying boats.

Edward Jablonski. The master aviation writer who donated many photographs from his own collection.

Roger W. Griswold II. He is currently flying a promising amphibian incorporating recent design developments, including many of his own.

Corwin H. Meyer. A Grumman vice-president and a senior experimental test pilot, who contributed to the chapters on operations.

Very special thanks and appreciation go to the following who were directly involved in this book.

Mrs. Eleanor Friede, my editor and a flyer herself, whose continuing advice and help started even before the first draft.
Wolfgang Langewiesche, another long-time friend whose flattering Introduction is a deep-felt honor.
Louise Kurt, my sweetheart, whose encouragement, sustained interest and gentle suggestions I see again on every page.
Marilyn Zimmerman, my helpful and ever-corrective Secretary.

My further appreciation goes to those friends in Washington who programmed my research.

Jean Ross Howard of the Aerospace Industries Association and President of the Whirly Girls.
David Scott of the Sport Aviation Association.
Stanley Green of the General Aviation Manufacturers Association.
John L. Baker, Assistant Administrator for General Aviation Affairs, Federal Aviation Administration.

And I offer a final bow and thanks to all whose names I have freely used in the many yarns of water flying lore.

INTRODUCTION

As Franklin T. Kurt points out in this book, there are more seaplanes flying now than ever before. You merely don't notice them much, because the seaplane has its being far from the crowded airports and noisy traffic patterns of suburbia. That is exactly its special charm—it frees you from the need for airports, it penetrates to the lakes and rivers, the resorts and the wilderness, and also to the downtown waterfronts. Possible water-landing areas are almost infinitely more numerous than airports are, and are plentiful even in dry sections of the country where reservoirs are numerous. Of all flying machines, the seaplane most nearly fulfills the dream of flying—beautiful and clean, free and relaxed.

Hank Kurt writes about seaplane flying with unique authority. At the age of five he decided to become not a locomotive engineer but a pilot. In 1925 he soloed, on a Navy single-float seaplane. He continued his training on big naval flying boats, was commissioned Ensign at 22. At 23 he graduated from MIT with a BS in aeronautical engineering. He is also a yachtsman and a life-long summer resident on his island in Maine, a region where the seaplane has always been important as a means of serious transportation.

To get practical experience, Kurt went from college immediately into commercial flying. At that time there were no airlines yet in the US. He barnstormed, on both landplanes and seaplanes, giving people rides. He gave Amelia Earhart, then a social worker in Boston, the refresher course she needed to get her first pilot's license. He then became a "fixed-base operator" at Hyannis on Cape Cod and at Boston. He designed the Kitty Hawk open-cockpit biplane, and with Allen Bourdou, had it certificated, and sold thirty-nine before the Great Depression closed in. He redesigned the French Schreck flying boat as an amphibian with an American engine, and in 1929 became Chief Engineer and Test Pilot for the Viking Flying Boat Company at New Haven, Connecticut. During the depression he kept flying by becoming the "Operator" of the New Haven airport. Many Yale men of that period learned flying from Franklin T. Kurt.

In the thirties, Franklin T. Kurt became well known among American pilots for his articles in *The Sportsman Pilot*, that large glossy monthly which was then the only voice of private flying. Mostly these articles reviewed the new airplanes. Today this is regular fare in the aviation magazines. Then, the idea was new. Hank Kurt brought to it the charm and sophistication of the theater critics of that period, whose reviews were often of more interest than the plays they talked about. For many of us, his articles put the airplane into perspective for the first time.

At that time, little was in print of much use to a pilot. The engineering books were written by nonpilots and did not show the piloting consequences of the engineering facts. Books written by pilots were addressed to the general public. The Army and Navy manuals were no help. Flying was not supposed to be learnable from words: you learned it by experience and feel.

But here came Franklin T. Kurt and wrote for the pilot. In urbane language, quite without jargon, quite without math, he connected for us cause and effect, engineering fact and flying behavior. What, for example, was "wing loading," what was "power loading," and what difference did those numbers make to the pilot? What was meant by the geometry of the landing gear, and how did it affect the way an airplane handled? What difference did aspect ratio make? Hank Kurt answered that one simply by saying that for a wing or propeller it was more efficient to push gently on a lot of air, than to push hard on a little air. One of the fundamentals of flight stated with elegant simplicity.

The present book is in the same style. Behind its easy language is deep understanding and solid experience. Kurt joined the Grumman Company and for many years was man-of-all-work about the famous Grumman amphibians. He tested them and demonstrated them to prospective customers, sold them and checked out the lucky owners, or their pilots, in handling them. Often he would pilot such an airplane for some owners on their first trips that extended to the tropics and deep into the Canadian bush.

Those amphibians—the Widgeon, the Goose, the Mallard—were perhaps the most desirable private airplanes ever built. The Goose had the speed of the airliners of its time and was at home on the big airports, yet could penetrate anywhere a small power boat could go. It could waddle out of the water onto the beach; hence, it could be parked on its owners' shorefront estate. Grumman owners and pilots lived in a little air age all their own, way ahead of the rest of the world. A Grumman Goose might take its owner to the Wall Street seaplane ramp in the morning, then make one or two more round trips between Long Island and midtown Manhattan on such missions as taking the children to the dentist; it would pick its owner up at Wall Street ramp in the evening, and on takeoff perhaps fly beneath the Brooklyn Bridge. (With a north or south wind, you had to.) And next day it might take him salmon fishing in Newfoundland. These airplanes were of course very expensive. But the essential thing they had, the power of penetration, can be had from any low-cost two-seat light plane on floats.

That's why a book on seaplane flying may have an important message for many pilots.

There is an extra reason why you will find this book useful. A seaplane on the water is really a boat. And boat handling is a skill that can be first understood best from a book. Practice will then develop judgment and skill all the faster.

Take riding: theory helps so little that no engineering analysis of the horse and rider system has ever been attempted, as far as I know. Take golf: reading helps but little; mostly, golf is a matter of kinesthetic practice. Take flying itself: theory helps a lot, but not at first. If a nonpilot took off alone, without a safety pilot, trusting his theoretic understanding, he would be in deep trouble right away. His senses would be confused. His attention would be overpowered by the rapid flow of events and disturbances. He would be disoriented and overwhelmed. Only with practice and habituation can he bring theoretical knowledge to bear on flying.

But boat handling is different. You can read up on sailing —once you have understood how a sailboat works and how the sailor thinks, you are ready for action. If you pick a gentle breeze and a simple boat, you can do an acceptable job of sailing right away.

The same applies to seaplane handling. Once you have clearly understood the forces acting upon a seaplane on the water—the weather-cocking effect of the wind, the relentless forward pull of the prop even when it is idling, the drift with the wind, the drift with the current, the effect of water rudder and of air rudder, the drag effect of the ailerons, the centrifugal force in turns, the heeling effect of cross-wind, lateral resistance in the water, the lift-force of the water on the underwater body, and so on—once you have seen them, you can deal with them. A good example is the fast upwind turn. It capsizes the unwary because the capsizing moment is much greater than generally expected. But to keep from being thrown, all you need is to know that this is so, and to take the turn at minimum speed.

Well, Hank Kurt discusses all these complex forces with the realism that comes from experience *and* theory. His discussion of waves and swells should put an end to the old saying that if you have seen one wave you've seen them all. His discussion of porpoising is something you won't find anywhere else. His diagram on page 47, showing how a pilot might maneuver on the water, should be an eye-opener: *that* is how the seaplane pilot thinks! Including the saucy note: "Next time land here."

So, when you read this book, it's not a case of reading about something which someday you may set out to learn. You are learning it, to a high degree, right as you read. The day you finally get out on the water you'll be amazed to find you know your way around pretty well, and you will realize you've had a good instructor.

—*Wolfgang Langewiesche*

PART ONE

Seaplane Flight: *Operations, Amphibian Basics*

1

EXTENT OF WATER FLYING

An airplane can be equipped to land on land, water, snow, or ice, but it is always an airplane for all that. If you are already a pilot, you are not entering a new profession when you undertake water flying; you are merely changing your mount. You are enlarging the basic potential of being an airman. There is far less to learn than when advancing from visual flight to instrument flight; you should have no more difficulty than a landlubber learning to sail. The lore and the law of the sea must be understood, just as you learned the ways of wind, clouds, and weather when first learning to fly.

Water flying brings a new sense of freedom, a release from restriction. It is like a return to the old days when precise navigation was unnecessary and skies were uncongested. Earphones remain on the hook, and you can chat freely with friends aboard. Flight plans, except in wild country, are unneeded. There are no precise approach or departure patterns, no estimated time of arrival or position-reporting after frantic computing. You fly relaxed and discover anew the enveloping beauty of nature.

DEFINITIONS

Dictionaries disagree on the relative classification of water-flying aircraft. Depending on which dictionary you refer to, the definitions fall into the following order:

Hydro airplanes (Hydro aeroplanes in England)
- flying boats
- seaplanes (here meaning only floatplanes)
- amphibians

or

Seaplanes
- flying boats
- floatplanes
- amphibians (which can be either flying boats or floatplanes)

In this book we will use the last order, but often the terms "floatplane" and "seaplane" will be used interchangeably to designate the same configuration.

"Configuration" is an engineer's term that means the general structural arrangement of the many components that make an airplane. It defines the relative location or relation of each assembly to the others. It may also relate to the general shape or contours.

With few exceptions, any airborne seaplane of any configuration flies like any other airplane. The techniques of takeoff and landing are slightly different but very simple. (What a strange misnomer that is: *land*ing! Rightfully it should be *sea*ing or *water*ing. In Newfoundland, they call it "pitch." Birds pitch in the trees, landplanes pitch on runways, and seaplanes pitch on the water.)

The real fun comes in applying good judgment and skill while maneuvering on the water. Then a seaplane *is* a boat, although a pretty cranky one, and subject to all the marine rules of the road. (Another misnomer.) More important, you are under strong obligation not to alarm or annoy people in other boats anchored, underway, or on shore. A throttled-down seaplane climbing gently out of a harbor entrance is never bothersome, but a full-power climbing turn out over a residential area will soon prevent others from landing in the harbor. Such a takeoff is rarely necessary.

By any judgment, a seaplane is a nasty boat. She has a beam (span) greater than her length! In a gusty wind she steers even more erratically than a beating sailboat. Though an experienced boat pilot can taxi safely through a very congested harbor under good conditions, he should usually terminate his taxiing out of such areas by choosing to stop in relatively open water with ample maneuvering room.

He can terminate his trip and secure his plane in a number of ways. Picking up a vacant mooring is the best. Or he can anchor. There are always small boys in a boat alongside even before the scope is payed out. They're always delighted to take your party ashore. It is easy to make a landing to a float, provided the ramp and any poles don't stick up higher than the wing that must pass over them. Low docks are equally good; but don't tie up at a low dock at high tide and go away! A slow cautious approach to a moored boat is good provided someone you know is aboard. Motorboats invariably yaw from side to side and elude your well-aimed upwind approach. The best way is to switch off and throw a line to the boat, slowly pulling your bow to her stern. If there is a seaplane ramp or a firm beach in the harbor, you have it made.

"THE WILD CATFISH"

A few floatplanes are less cranky on floats than on wheels. I was fortunate enough to make the first test flights of a Wildcat seaplane. As World War II penetrated deeper into the South Pacific, the Japanese mounted Zero fighters on floats to afford protection in island areas where there were no flight strips. The United States needed fighters to counter them, and the Navy hurriedly started to convert a hundred Wildcats to floats. She was nicknamed "the Wild Catfish." What else? Only two were ever assembled, because the Sea Bees constructed island airstrips so fast, even under fire, that the seaplane fighters were never needed.

The Wildcat, the early World War II Navy fighter, was midwing, with an extremely narrow landing gear raised and lowered laboriously by hand crank. We factory pilots were experienced with flying boats, which lean first on one wing-tip float, then on the other, and the Wildcat's tendency to lean during a crosswind landing bothered us not at all. We never thought they were bad ground loopers. (A ground loop is an uncontrolled swerve off the runway.) But the Navy landplane pilots soon experienced a rash of severe ground

The Wild Catfish—W.W. II Grumman F4F on Edo floats. (Edo Aircraft)

loops. The crosswind component caused them to lean toward the downwind side during a landing runout. The midwing, seemingly at collar level on either side of the cockpit, afforded a nearby sighting level, making the tilt look worse than it really was. It alarmed the Navy boys, who were precise pilots, and they would apply full aileron to bring up the low wing. Also, because they were good pilots, they "coordinated" the controls and instinctively pushed rudder at the same time, which caused the violent swerve company pilots had avoided.

The wing loading and the landing speed of the "Wild Catfish" was as high as the Schneider Cup Racers' of fifteen years earlier. They had a reputation for being extremely nervous airplanes. For both these reasons I approached the first "Wild Catfish" flight, not with fear, but with extreme caution. However, I'd overlooked the Edo utility floats with nearly 100 percent reserve buoyancy, whereas the record breakers had only about 60 percent, demanding all the pilot's skill. To my great pleasure, those huge floats, which slowed down the fighter woefully, made her an old man's airplane. I could literally throw her at the water in the most careless landings, wing low, in a skid, too fast, or in a high dropout, and the floats would accept the plane as if on two big cushions and say, "Relax, boy—I've gotcha!" No airport surface or landing gear would be that good.

WHY WATER FLYING?

In the late twenties, the Italian Commander Francisco de Pinedo made many brilliant long-range flights in flying boats. When he was asked why he did not use landplanes, he replied, "When I fly some new-where and look down at land, I see fields and I no know whether field is rough or soft or plant to crop, but when I look down and see water, I know water is water ever'where."

There was another good reason why he used flying boats —they were then capable of longer-range flights than landplanes. Giant airports had not yet been envisioned. Seaplanes had three- or even ten-mile smooth takeoff runs in any harbor all over the world. If flying boats had enough thrust to plow through the critical 20-knot "hump speed," they could accelerate a terrific overload of fuel into flight with an unlimited take-off run.

This was the golden decade of water flying. Britain, the United States, Italy, and France were competing annually in the Schneider Cup Races for the world's maximum speed record. The airplanes with the smallest wings and the fastest takeoff speed were naturally the leading contenders. Here again, there were no airports long enough and smooth enough to get them safely airborne. Only water flying could advance the science of aerodynamics.

For water flying, both these achievements—longer range and new high-speed records—were a self-defeating advance. Landplanes soon required equal takeoff facilities, which began the endless parade towards ever larger airports.

2

SCOPE OF WATER FLYING

STATISTICS

There are now more floatplanes, flying boats, and amphibians in civil use than ever before. Although steadily growing in popularity, the growth rate is less than for landplanes. The ratio decreases as landplanes and helicopters of all sizes and purposes multiply like rabbits, and waterborne aircraft become a smaller percentage of the total. Although logic would say there should be a firm relationship between the number of airplanes and the landing places they use, the number of available United States airports has changed little in the past five years, holding at about 12,000.

The airport situation may have a direct bearing on the growth of seaplanes. As frequent airline travelers know, there are four big-city terminal airports already saturated with airliner traffic, causing tedious delays. Only about 800 of the recognized airports have control towers and instrument approach facilities. Even fewer are served by regularly scheduled airlines. The remaining 11,000 or so serve the great general aviation fleet. A few of these are approaching saturation, and most of them are becoming crowded with rows of staked-down personal and small business airplanes. More airports are urgently needed, but the infernal noise of aviation is driving them farther from population centers, nearly all of which are located on water courses.

Seaplanes are also dogged with the noise problem. Many lakes are closed to seaplane operation. Nevertheless, most of the 500 or so recognized seaplane bases have been operating a long time and have proved acceptable to their neighbors. Many more individual seaplanes operate off-base wherever the owner wishes. He seldom cares or needs to report his facility as a "base."

The scope of all United States aircraft operations should be listed as background before extracting seaplane statistics. At the end of 1972 there were approximately 700,000 licensed pilots. There were over 135,000 registered aircraft. Special groups within this number, in round figures, are:

4200 VTOL helicopters: 2000 commercial
750 corporate
450 police and government
3000 sport—homebuilt airplanes
ineligible for commercial use
2700 airliners: 2400 on domestic routes
300 on overseas routes
200 sailplanes (gliders)
30 balloons and dirigibles

It is difficult to secure accurate statistics on the number of seaplanes now flying. Figures for the United States are confused because many airplanes are floatplanes in summer and landplanes in winter. Furthermore, when amphibians within the continental US come up for resale, two out of three are snapped up for export to frontier-type countries. For example, of 276 Widgeons built, only 104 were registered in this country in mid-1972. In late 1972, Federal Aviation Administration data showed 1400 seaplanes were regularly operated from seaplane bases. About 1800 were flying in Alaska and from random individual locations, bringing the US seaplane fleet to approximately 2400. At least 300 are flying in Canada, and although little data is available for the rest of the world, there are many seaplanes in the East Indies and Scandinavian countries, a scattering in Central and South America, and a few in Africa and Australia. We can safely conclude that the world seaplane fleet exceeds the number of transports in the US airline fleet.

By adding the number of seaplanes to the 13,500 totaled in the special groups listed above, and deducting from the total registry of 135,000, the remaining general aviation fleet used for personal, small business, and commerce totals about 120,000 airplanes. No wonder our limited number of airports are becoming overcrowded!

UTILITY

Flying from water is a practical, logical, and useful way to make airplanes "work" for you. A trip by landplane from departure to destination involves: (1) an automobile trip, (2) an airport (meaning delay), (3) a flight, (4) another airport, (5) another automobile trip. Most trips by seaplane involve only: (1) a short walk, (2) a flight, (3) another short walk! In contrast to the 12,000 airports, an infiinite number of sheltered bodies of water rim our coastline and the Great Lakes. There are many thousands of miles of navigable rivers. Most of the nation is studded with beautiful lakes. There have been hundreds of pure seaplane flights from coast to coast across prairies and mountains.

Most villages, towns, and cities, the objectives of most trips, are on waterways because they were originally settled and supplied there by water traffic. Ready-made landing areas, smooth, large, and with more adjacent facilities than airports, exist right at their front door.

There are no air navigation facilities permitting instrument flights—truly a serious handicap—but contact flying under low clouds and limited visibility is far safer than over land. There is a real hazard from high-tension lines across rivers, but these are now generally marked with highly visible balls or can be easily noted on flight charts. They are much less of a hazard than high towers and other obstructions when flying low over land, a method used only by small utility airplanes anyway.

Why is water flying not more popular? Perhaps because it is easier to train a good seaman to become an accomplished air pilot than to train a pilot in the ways of the sea. This is a costly factor. Insurance rates for seaplanes are more than for equivalent landplanes. Seaplanes suffer more frequent small damage and are even destroyed more often in water-handling episodes than airplanes operating on airports.

The closest I ever came to utterly demolishing a beautiful Mallard amphibian plane was on a lovely day in calm water at almost zero speed. Six of us were going salmon fishing on a sparkling blue lake deep in high, green mountains far out in the Newfoundland bush. After circling the lake several times, I decided not to anchor and go ashore in the inflatable dinghy, but to nose up gently to the shore. I selected a beach near the lake outlet.

While taxiing slowly toward the shore, I chose not to lower the landing gear as a buffer on the bottom because the gravel beach appeared too rough to permit taxiing out onto it. So I nosed the ship in very slowly to prevent the sharp stones from scratching the hull upon grounding. This meant "blipping" the engine switches to attain the slowest possible approach. Things were pretty busy in the cockpit, and each time I looked ahead to check the intended landing point, it seemed always a bit farther to the right. About then it was time to look overboard and make sure there were no larger

Hooking a Newfoundland salmon. Grumman Mallard.

outlying rocks. To my amazement and horror the bottom was sliding underneath at a pretty fast clip. Glancing to port, I noticed only then that we were at the narrowing entrance of the forgotten lake outlet and were being sucked into it at an ever faster pace. Not 300 feet downstream there were foaming rock-studded rapids that could grind the beautiful Mallard to pieces forever!

I gunned the engines and turned away from the beach in a shower of silver spray. It was then easy to effect a beach landing some 800 feet farther to the right, where there was no current.

How did we get off safely? If an engine failed to start after we left shore, the rapids were still not far away. I walked back on the deck of the hull and dropped an anchor off the tail into deep water, passing the line under the wing to the bow cleat. The last man to board over the nose pushed us off, and we were soon riding to the anchor, tail to the rapids. As soon as both engines were idling smoothly, we lifted the anchor aboard through the bow hatch as the boat overran it.

No insurance claim that day! Just as in all other phases of flying, experience teaches prudent water operations.

FUN

Is increased utility a seaplane's only worth? Certainly not. Flying purely for fun is a fully justified reward, and you will find new fun in flying from, to, and over the water. Many spend more on winter skiing, which has no "utility" at all.

Only the airman can observe the full beauty and limitless expanse of all nature. Under VFR conditions he flies immersed in the glory of ever-changing scenery, superlative when it is half land, half water. The single-engine landplane owner may hesitate to prowl around low in the rugged barren area of Lake Powell on the Colorado River. The amphibian owner gets right down in it. Low flight seems natural, safe, and logical.

Flying low, we observe more interesting sights more intimately. Upon landing, we are immediately immersed in the active life of the waterfront. We see and meet a variety of people, in sharp contrast to the confined and remote activities of isolated airports. Shorelines where the land meets the sea hold a strong fascination for everyone, always changing, ever new.

FLYING A COASTLINE

Ah, the serene sheer joy of flying a curving coastline! At one time or another over a period of 42 years, I have flown every mile of coastline from Detroit along both sides of Lake

Erie, Lake Ontario, the St. Lawrence River, around the Gaspé Peninsula, and both coasts of Nova Scotia; every mile of the Atlantic Coast and the Gulf of Mexico from Eastport, Maine to Mérida, Yucatan. I flew the Pacific Coast of Central America from Tehuantepec to Panama, thence around the Caribbean, low and close all around the beautiful islands of Jamaica, most of the Cuban shores, and back to Key West. For years I never closed the gap between St. Petersburg and Havana. (Ultimately the day came, but that flight was disappointingly high at 10,000 feet.)

Flying the Bahama Islands is now familiar to many landplane pilots. They are easy, wonderful, gorgeous, colorful, exotic when seen through any windshield, but never so good as from a seaplane landing to a gleaming silver beach in transparent water.

Much of this mileage was flown below 1000 feet and most of it only a few feet over the surf line. Have you ever flown the Texas beaches? Longhorn steers browsing near the cool of the beach take off like antelope as you approach. Long-legged Texas jackrabbits attempt to bound ahead only to dart inshore as you swoop over, their leaps so long they seem to sail like birds. When landing at Houston after that flight, the ship was white with encrusted salt from the mist above the surf line. It took an hour to hose off.

I flew with Dick Light in his Bellanca floatplane along the majestic coast of the Gaspé Peninsula about 500 feet up and 500 feet out from the nearly sheer cliffs towering well above us, then down to the water to look through the natural arch of Perce Rock. A few minutes later as we flew across the Baie des Chaleurs at 100 feet, a whale spouted ahead. We nosed down sharply; the whale sounded, and the spray from his flukes lapped the floats. At sunset we landed in the fishy-woody-smelling village of Chatham and slept that night in a front room of a century-old hostelry with the Bellanca nodding at a mooring only a few hundred feet away. The next morning we chased the frightening bore wave up the Moncton River. Later, in 1933, Dick flew that Bellanca seaplane around the world except for the leg from Tokyo to Seattle made aboard a vessel.

One chill, hazy, overcast day in November I landed a party at a duck blind in Currituck Sound. The glassy water reflected the gray sky. Using the blind as a point of reference to judge the flaring height, we kissed the water, expecting to drop off the step about at the blind. I passed it at flying speed and went and went! Obviously, the water was bare inches deep over a slippery mudbank. We even overran again when turning back, but no loaded seaplane ever made a shorter takeoff!

ADVENTURE

I've chased a hurricane around the Gulf of Mexico in the New York *Daily News* Mallard amphibian. The photographers secured excellent news photographs showing ghastly damage along the Biloxi coast. Although the storm had passed, waters were still rising fast at the New Orleans Moisant Airport. The field was already closed, with water lapping the runways. With a laugh the tower let us land because we were an amphibian. It was a wheeled landing on the runway, but we departed later as a seaplane from the flooded grassy part of the field.

We returned to Mobile over the offshore islands hoping to find further news items. At Cat Island an abandoned, husky Customs Service boat floated safely in a cove partly filled. A few miles farther the Ship Island Customs Base was badly mauled, with every wooden structure washed away except the sturdy Army-type barracks. It too was badly damaged. We saw no one on the first pass but swept back to take pictures and then saw ladies' panties flying from a line! There's life there, a news item—maybe cheesecake too! Those on the other side of the ship spotted an American flag flying upside down, while on the left side a large sign tramped into the sand appealed for HELP!

A large pier had been swept away with only a few pilings left projecting above water. I taxied in cautiously between two upended Jeeps almost submerged well out from the beach. When the keel lightly scraped the murky sand, we all went overboard in our briefs, set the anchor, and waded in carrying cameras over our heads. There were four men and two badly shaken ladies waiting on the beach. They had barely escaped the fury during the night but were unhurt, though hungry and still frightened. One was a diabetic in urgent need of insulin. The disconsolate shipkeeper, only months away from retirement, had a perfect record until his boat was lost from her mooring during the blow. His dull eyes lighted up marvelously when he learned she was still

A Customs Service shipkeeper finds his lost vessel after a Gulf of Mexico hurricane. Author is in cockpit. (*N.Y. Daily News*)

afloat. And could we take him to her to erase the smirch on his record? Although he had seen us wade ashore without trouble, he almost balked at wading back to the amphib. Didn't we know that the water was alive with water moccasins washed out of the loblolly pines after every hurricane?

We put him aboard, flew to Mobile, and reported to the Customs Office, who sent us food, insulin, and other supplies to take back to the island with the news that a boat would be sent out for them the next day.

3

ADVANTAGES OF WATER FLYING

SAFETY

Seaplanes have many unique safety features. They afford an opportunity to "stop flying gracefully," as the barnstormers used to say. Over sheltered water you may stop flying anywhere—suddenly. Weather shut-in or engine failure causes no panic. Come down and land easily where you are. Possible landing hazards are easily seen and avoided. Although deep-sea forced landings may lead to some damage, they provide greater safety than ditching a landplane.

If a seaplane suffers a forced landing over land, it can be brought down on its bottom with assurance. Usually no damage occurs in a smooth field—only a few dents, at worst. If the terrain is rough and rocky, the hull will take severe damage before the cabin is affected. The floats and struts of a floatplane will crumple progressively, providing excellent emergency shock absorbers. Seaplane pilots in mountainous country feel more secure than in a landplane. Bush pilots consider a single-engine seaplane safer than a twin-engine landplane.

Nowadays, almost all land flying is from narrow runways, usually involving a crosswind component. Open field operations permitting takeoff in any direction or in a curve are very rare. Seldom do seaplanes land crosswind. They may make curving landings or takeoffs under greater control on the yielding water surface than on a hard runway. (This technique will be discussed in Chapter 5 under "Crosswind Technique.")

Another little item, better labeled "comfort," falls under "safety." How many times have you squirmed and writhed during the last half hour of a flight in a small airplane yearning to empty your bladder but unable to find an airport en route? It happens, and maybe the discomfort has a bearing on safety, one way or another. When flying a coastline or lake district, it's no problem. Just throttle back, land anywhere, and make yourself comfortable!

AMPHIBIANS

The versatility, and hence safety, of amphibians greatly exceeds that of pure seaplanes. (These aspects will be elaborated in Chapter 10.) Refueling at water bases is now uncommon, although prior to World War II, one of my pleasantest midday stops was at a Pan American raft in the harbor of Antigua Island. Customs approved our entry by a conversation with a dignified Negro who spoke elegant English and referred to me as "Marster," as on any ship. There ensued a pleasant snack lunch in the warm Caribbean sunshine while fuel was pumped aboard. There are no such convenient bases today.

In contrast, there was an amphibian landing at Montego Bay, Jamaica, after the war. Fuel facilities at the flight strip were undergoing improvement, necessitating a full day's delay. An easy hop into the harbor and landing at an old dock that surely dated back to the days of Morgan the pirate solved the problem. Laughing townspeople rolled out aviation fuel drums stored on the wharf. We used our

Spencer Amphibian Air Car. Over 25 are under construction by home builders of the Sport Aviation Association. (Percival Spencer)

own funnel and chamois cloth to strain the gasoline and soon rounded up a line of stark naked Jamaican boys who brought five-gallon drums aboard by stepping onto the wing tip and then to the center section tanks. The gleeful boys threw the empty cans ashore and departed over the tail and stabilizer back to the dock. Because of amphibian versatility, we were soon underway south with no overnight delay.

Of course, amphibians usually accept the convenience of refueling at airports. Also, when there is a hurricane threatening, they may be housed safely in hangars. However, securing a seaplane to a good mooring in a sheltered harbor is another safe way to weather a hurricane. She will lie nose into the wind and, unlike tethered landplanes, never snatch at the restraining lines.

It is hard to believe there ever was a day when wing loadings were as light as six pounds per square foot. However, in the twenties I observed an Aeromarine single-float seaplane with enormous biplane wings at a mooring in a full gale. For security the mooring pennant had been passed around the two forward float struts, forming a yoke. The projected line of the pennant passed so close to the center of gravity that she repeatedly took off and flew like a kite. Though the owner was summoned by telephone, he arrived after the seaplane finally fell in on one wing and was rather badly damaged. There is no such worry with modern highly wing-loaded seaplanes at moorings.

Back in the thirties, Erik Hofman, a life-long friend, and Mundy Peale, later president of Republic Aircraft, were flying a Sikorsky S–39 single-engine amphibian to an air meet at Sioux City, Iowa. It was a slow flight bucking strong headwinds, and only an amphibian would have made it that day. Fuel was running dangerously low. There was a nest of thunderstorms as they approached the city. When they sighted the airport at last, a torrential rain cut them off. So they landed on the Missouri River near the airport and anchored to wait it out.

The rains continued. The river rose, and the current became too strong to haul in the snagged anchor when the airport at last opened up. Both men stripped naked and went into shoulder-deep water to clear the fouled anchor. After some effort, it came free, and they swarmed aboard, Erik to fly and Mundy to retrieve the anchor and line before they drifted onto a sandbar.

It was fast work, particularly because another thunder bumper threatened to close the airport again. They roared off and barely lowered the wheels in time to make the runway lined along the edge with a crowd of farmers' families. As the tail came down, the Sikorsky ran out of gas! It was a strange craft to be seen in prairieland, and the crowd rushed out to look in the windows as the stark naked crew struggled desperately to dress their dripping bodies.

LEARNING ON WATER

Initial flight instruction in seaplanes is simpler than in landplanes. Synthesis of the learning process makes it easier. Each new sequential step should be separated from those preceding and following. Confusion results when they become simultaneous or in too rapid sequence. A beginning student who has naturally made all his previous spatial movements in close visual relation to his surroundings becomes lost when he simultaneously attempts to maneuver an airplane around three axes using three new controls. If he first undertakes this novel effort close enough to the ground to receive visual aid, it will be simplified.

AIR WORK

I learned to fly in the US Navy on surplus World War I Curtiss N–9 single-float seaplanes. Extra wing area and span provided the lift needed to compensate for the added engine and float weight. The trussing cell between the interplane struts of a biplane was called a "bay." The N–9s had three bays on each side instead of the usual two.

Curtiss Navy N-9 with Hisso engine; a seagoing three-bay Jennie. The author's first solo, 1925.

Slow and sluggish, they responded poorly to the ailerons and rolled ponderously. At the end of the second instruction hour I was still skidding the turns. My desperate instructor, Reggie Thomas, ordered me to fly at very low altitude and hold precisely over the winding southern coastline of Boston Harbor. Oh boy, I learned fast! The ship didn't contour the curving coastline but drifted annoyingly either offshore or far inland. I then caught on quickly, soon wrapping the course tightly around each headland and concave cove with bank angles that felt surprisingly correct to the seat of the pants. N–9s flew woefully slowly, and there were no airspeed or turn and bank indicators then. Turns were extremely tight with a very short radius. The hard work of learning to fly terminated that day. Thereafter, every minute of instruction was exhilarating fun.

Airplanes in those days were novel and relatively quiet by today's standards. Shore residents rarely objected; they usually came out to wave. There were only a few who angrily called our skipper, the revered Commander Noel Davis. It was an education to hear him tactfully field the call by explaining gently that their slight annoyance was materially assisting the US Navy in preparing for a war with Japan! That was in 1925. It seemed a ridiculous statement then, but many of my classmates lived and flew to give their lives over the South Pacific seventeen years later fighting the Japanese.

LANDINGS AND TAKEOFFS

Initial landing instruction on airports defies an orderly synthesis. There should be separate lessons on approach glide speed, glide angle to the desired landing spot, judgment of height, when and how much to flare, and allowance for crosswinds. Unfortunately, these all have to be learned, if not simultaneously, at least in rapid succession. When a takeoff and complete circuit means a full four minutes before another attempt is made, the previous experience becomes stale.

Landing instruction in seaplanes permits easy separation of each problem, and even a continuous series of landings only twenty seconds apart. Made almost as frequently as baseball pitching practice, this procedure affords immediate correction of errors. The seaplane student determines the wind direction by a glance at the wave pattern and eliminates crosswind problems. He experiments to determine optimum power-off glide speed without worry about accuracy at the touchdown point. He is directed to fly into the wind at minimum power speed at fifteen feet above the water, then ten feet, then at five feet. The instructor sharpens his judgment of height above the surface by an occasional up–down signal. A two- or three-mile pass requires no more than four minutes, but a few such passes provide a continuous experience that a landplane student gets only in snatches at each landing extending over two or three hours.

With this exercise embedded in the student's perception, the instructor proceeds to actual landings. In another long pass the throttle is closed at sufficient altitude, perhaps 300 feet, to allow the student to establish the glide, and in a series of takeoffs and landings he learns to flare and touch down. There is an immediate takeoff and climb with ensuing landings every sixty to ninety seconds, permitting three or four in quick series—more if the length of the harbor or lake permits.

Next, a buoy is selected as a target to make spot landings. The instructor will have the student land on either side alternately to assure that he doesn't form a habit of judging by looking out only one side. When he becomes proficient in touching water precisely at the buoy, the student is told to touch at an estimated spot so that the landing runout terminates at the buoy. Then a long run is made up the shore with the instructor indicating a variety of targets—off a point, near anchored boats, in a narrow channel—thus broadening the student's adaptation to varied approaches, a practice that serves him well on later landplane flying.

How often does a landplane student come out to the airport only to find the runway crosswind is too brisk for his next logical lesson? This never happens on the water. His crosswind lesson takes only one hour. He is directed to first land only a little off the wind, and in succeeding touchdowns he works up gradually to the maximum crosswind component that the particular airplane and conditions permit. Furthermore, in the same lesson he learns to adapt to winds from *either* side.

There are many advantages in taking initial instruction and solo on the water. Lesser cost is the most important. It requires fewer hours to the first solo, and the student has acquired more basic experience when he reaches that point.

4

RUDIMENTS

HOW IT'S GOING TO BE

Anyone can fly off and back onto the water—and get ashore again. Fun begins on the first flight, and unlike learning instrument flying, there's no hard work involved.

The path to ultimate good judgment and skill is simply the amassing of experience. After a short checkout period you will be soloed and can gather experience on your own if you are cautious and ask for frequent checkouts.

There are five basic precepts:

1. Observe—observe—observe—observe.
2. Think—analyze—verify.
3. Plan ahead—replan.
4. Execute.
5. Abandon—and try again.

That fifth step is the easy out. Many experienced seaplane pilots will start a landing only to observe something new and take off to try a better one, perhaps some other place. You are never confined to a runway. There are no tower traffic controllers watching and ordering you around. Like other web-footed pilots, you will make approaches or perhaps taxi to a dock, only to turn away and elect to come in at a different and better angle. Strangely, you will find very little happens suddenly. On the water there is usually time to reconsider and then do it better.

Primary flight instructors have often noted that the most adaptive students are those who have sailed or ridden horseback. Sailors are familiar with fluid motions and are used to yielding, rather than positive, controls. It is difficult to explain why horsemen are so apt, but it's probably because they sense the horse has a will of his own and they guide him more than command him. A seaplane has a definite character and will of its own too. When you try to make her go where you wish on the water, you'll find it best to cooperate. Let her have her own head.

Don't think you must be a sailor first. Even cowboys pick it up quickly. You'll please your checkout instructor and gain a little on flight time if you previously learn that left is *port* and right is *starboard.* Let's try it again: Port is *left.* Starboard is *right.* You should learn to tie a square knot (never a granny), a clove- or double half-hitch, and a bowline (see figure 1).

If you start flying on the coast, you'll give your checkout pilot confidence when you taxi into the seaplane base leaving red buoys on your starboard side, because you have learned "*R*ed to *R*ight *R*eturning," and black buoys on your port side. Reverse the rule when you leave. That's all.

In this school syllabus all seaplanes will be treated alike, because essentially they are. They do vary in configuration, and the differences will be highlighted when they affect a maneuver. The differences involve:

Catamarans (floatplanes)	Twin engine
Single hulls (flying boats)	Amphibians
Single engine	Reversible propellers

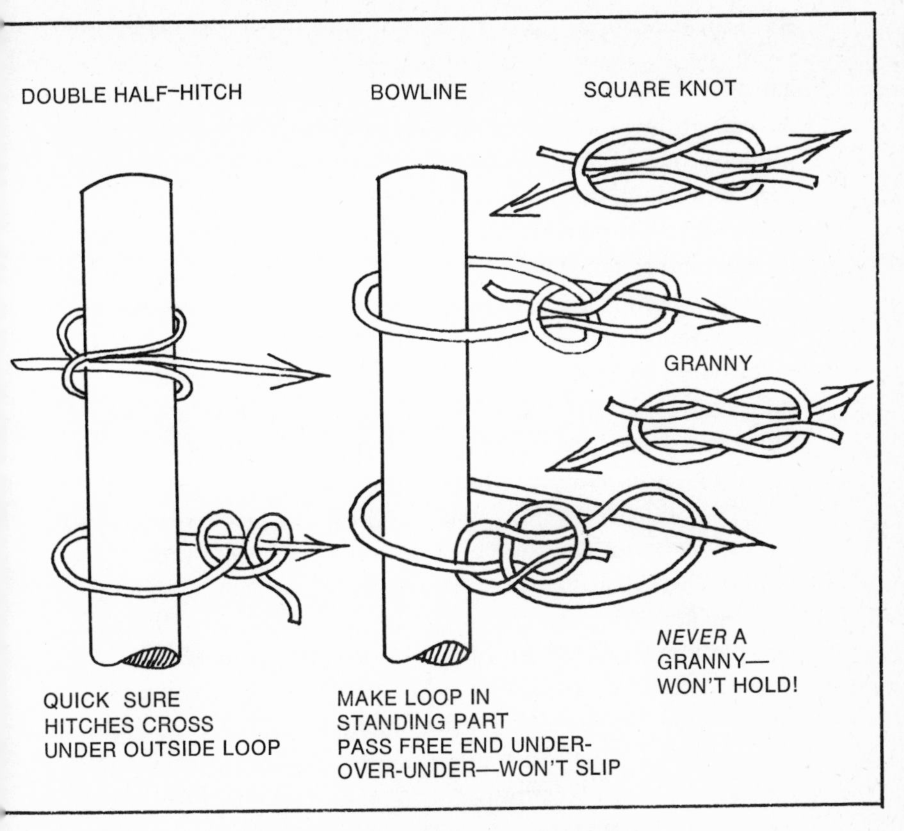

Figure 1—Three Essential Knots

Twin-engine seaplanes, amphibians, and those with reversible props have extra control capability on the water and will be so noted.

FIRST FLIGHT—A BIT STRANGE

Seaplane bases abound. Perhaps there is one within walking distance of the center of your town. Maybe it will be a short way up a little river flowing into the harbor or lake.

There will be a hangar with a broad apron at the top of a narrow ramp and a half dozen or so small twin-float seaplanes parked on their keels. Let's rent one, and make your first flight together. A mechanic wangles the ship onto a small wheeled platform by alternately tipping it on curved blocks under the keels. Maybe it already is mounted on axles projecting through open-ended tubes inside each float and having a pair of wheels located about under the center of gravity. In either case, it is pushed to the head of the ramp and tilted on blocks until it again rests on the keels. If the seaplane weighs much over 2500 pounds, more elaborate handling equipment is required.

After the usual preflight check, climb aboard and start the engine. Looking way down at the surface of the ramp, you'll think we're on stilts—because we are! Someone scoops up a few buckets of water from the river and throws them on the planking ahead for lubrication. I gun the engine, the mech rocks the tail up and down, and suddenly we start to slide. I yank the throttle back to make the slide more sedate, and chuckle as you push against the back of the seat as the nose tilts down alarmingly. It soon bobs up to level as the floats enter the water.

You will feel a bit uneasy and all adrift—because you are! The wind is blowing upriver, and the tide is flowing downriver. Now you quickly learn the difference between *heading, course,* and *track.* Heading is merely where we are pointing and is quite irrelevant. Course is where we are going, which is most important. Track is where we have been, and is useful to observe behind in order to plan ahead.

We're moving out into the stream and instinctively you push on the brakes in an attempt to stop and figure things out. But the brakes don't work—there aren't any! The light wind points us downstream but moves us upstream. The current moves us downstream, but doesn't point us anywhere. You'll look back and discover our track is astonishing. We are actually moving upstream while headed down!

You look bewildered, especially since the rudder feels ineffectual, but I come to your rescue by lowering a handle under the instrument board. There is a light snatch on the rudder pedals as the water rudders take over, and simultaneously I open the throttle. Now you have control. Taxiing out between the leafy banks beats any runway. In a moment we leave the river. A buoy lies ahead. I'm talking a lot about the forces acting to determine our course and seem unaware there is a boat coming from the opposite direction to round the same buoy. You get excited. You're not used to seeing boats—on the runway! We beat the boat to the buoy, but she's still bearing down on us, so I blast the engine. The bow climbs up. Spray flies underneath but, blessedly, you see us turn on a dime and pass the boat so fast it might as well have been anchored. Ahead lies a whole beautiful harbor larger than any airport, and at last you smile. You seem to feel freer than you ever felt in any airplane on the ground.

I ask you to taxi in circles to warm up the engine and ask you where the wind is. There are little confused waves everywhere and they seem at first to give no indication. But as you circle and see them from all angles, you find it easy to note their direction and hence that of the wind. You have *observed*—first precept.

Now we are ready and I make the first takeoff with you following me through on the controls, just as in initial instruction. Before full power, I retract the water rudders; no need for them when the air rudder is now fully effective in the slipstream. Besides, they bang up and down unless lifted out of the water. The bows pitch well up, you can hear and feel the spray purling under the fuselage and feel the small snatches on the pedals as it hits the air rudder. The little ship struggles for a moment but then seems to accelerate faster as the nose drops to a normal angle, and I let the wheel move forward. We're "on the step," and you smile, watching the spray streak behind.

Suddenly you're frightened as some ducks fly off the water ahead, but you marvel as I make a smooth, pretty sharp turn away from them, a sharper turn than we ever could make on land. You relax. The nose lowers a little more and the ship feels a bit sluggish. Instinctively, you pull the wheel back a little and glance at me to find I've taken my hands off. You pull a little more, and with a gentle nod she flies off. *Whee*!

You climb for altitude and feel perfectly at home except for the appearance of that big float flying along a few feet below your side. At 600 feet, I signal to level off. You circle the bay, seeing things below you never noticed before. Again you are *observing*. After a few minutes I suddenly pull the throttle back and suggest you take her down. But you feel you're not yet ready for *that*. So you look at me apprehensively, open the throttle again, and circle. Instead of bawling you out I just smile. You look at the water, see a sailboat, observe the wind direction, and note there are mud flats upwind. So you fly back a couple of miles, turn upwind, and look my way again to see a broader approving smile. In the absence of a prepared airport, you have *thought*, *analyzed*, and *verified*—the second precept. I again close the throttle and signal for a landing. You have *planned*—third precept.

O.K. Down you go. When it comes time to flare, the texture of the little waves tells you how high you are, and just when you think you've made it perfectly, you touch much earlier than expected. There is no bounce. Instead, the ship dips down and slides smoothly along the surface, slowing rapidly. Instinctively you hold the wheel back, especially when the spray off the bows moves forward and she settles in off the step with a small *whoosh.*

"That was perfect," I say, "except you forgot you were on stilts. Remember, the float bottoms are three feet lower than wheels." You have *executed*—fourth precept.

You forget you have an appointment. You fly and fly, until I wave you home. You never knew touch-and-go's could be so thrilling. You spot the buoy off the river, cut the throttle, and head for a landing precisely in the invisible wake of our first takeoff. But *whoa*! As you near the water you sense we are drifting sideways. The more you correct, the worse the crabbing angle becomes. You give her the gun and climb up for another look. Ah ha! The wave action around the buoy shows you the wind has changed 90 degrees. While I laugh, you sheepishly make a correct approach, though you know I'm laughing with approval. You have *abandoned* and *tried again*—fifth precept. All in one lesson, and what's more, you did it all yourself!

The wind is across the curving river and downwind to the ramp, the tide is dropping, the current faster, and you're mighty glad when I take over to taxi in. Oh well, something to learn the next time. You have a hundred questions, and ask what the difference would have been if the ship were a small flying boat.

"Just the same on the flying, landing, and takeoff, but it will look different. Taxiing out, the water will be about at seat level and look mighty close. You'll think there's much more spray because it covers the windshield going on the step. When she finishes the run and settles off the step, you'll think you're sinking. You might dislike tilting from one tip float to the other, but when taxiing on the step you can actually bank the turns with the ailerons to make even sharper turns. On the first landing you would probably drop her in because the bottom is nearer your seat than on wheels.

If she were an amphibian you'd find slow taxiing much easier because you could lower the wheels and slow her down by half. It's a darn sight easier to get her out of the water into the hangar, too."

Now you're hooked on water flying, and I leave you in the hands of the local instructor.

LANDINGS—AS ALWAYS

You will be safe to solo on water under good wind and sea conditions in a very few check flights, but it is well—and saves you rental money—if you press on with the instructor to gain more knowledge. Although experience is gained on all matters every minute you fly, probably he will concentrate on the little quirks in a helpfully logical sequence.

Landings are the simplest. They are made precisely as in a landplane. The airplane should be set down at its *minimum flying speed.* Make a power-off approach, except to clear out the engine, and flare as usual. Keep looking, but concentrate on the point ahead at which you expect to touch down, from 300 feet to 100 feet. Don't look directly down any more than you would on land. The uniformity of small wave patterns may give less clue to height than the edge of a runway with boundary lights, but if you're looking ahead you make this judgment by observing the whole water surface out to the horizon.

Touch down "three points" as you would with a tail-dragger landplane with the nose pretty well up. Keep the wheel coming back, if it isn't already all the way back. The tail of the floats and the step will then touch simultaneously. The pitch angle during runout will approximate that of a tricycle landing gear, not a tail-dragger. The water resistance on the bottom will slow her down sooner, and at that point, with the stick fully back to reduce spray, she will settle off the step.

Many pilots tend to drag the approach with a little power. On land, they keep a reserve for late and accurate adjustment to land just over the runway threshold. There is no need of this on the water. The touchdown point is less important. Still, keep a hand on the throttle. More will be said about this when we discuss glassy water conditions.

Several factors dictate minimum-speed landings. In the first place, the amount of wing area of any airplane was originally designed to produce a low enough landing speed to meet the intended operating conditions. If cruise instead of landing were the basic design parameter, wings would have less than half the area and span, resulting in much higher top speed. It is wise for a pilot to always land at the minimum speed in order to take advantage of all the available lift the designer intended. Unless the airplane has very poor control at landing speed, nothing is gained by touching down faster. On land, brake wear is more severe, and on water, a longer-than-necessary run results. In any case, a faster-than-minimum landing becomes tolerable only when the runway, or water surface, is so smooth that the airplane won't be bounced back into the air, requiring the pilot to land all over again. So, especially on rough water, full-stall landings are essential.

Second, the water forces produced by a hull sliding over the water increase as the *square of the speed.* A landplane on first contact receives very little backward force from the rolling wheels. A seaplane, however, instantly picks up a rearward force from the hull drag, which may lead to disconcerting change in trim. Hence, low speed is again important.

Third, some pilots, particularly beginners, find the uniformity of wave patterns tends to impair their judgment of altitude at the flare-out. If that is the case, it is better to err on the high side than the low, because if you drop in from a short distance at minimum speed, no harm is done other than a gentle bounce. Dropping from four feet onto a water surface is less severe than dropping four feet onto a runway. If contact is made lower or earlier, it is also faster, and the airplane may then fly off, requiring a whole new flare-out and landing.

Wind direction should be determined after careful study, since the pilot does not have the help of wind socks or airport radio operators. If there is no current, boats at anchor will point into the wind. Flags, smoke, whitecaps, the direction in which seagulls or other waterfowl are landing and taking off, the set of sails on sailboats, are all good indicators. If there is nothing else visible to indicate from which quarter the wind is blowing, the airplane may be flown close to the water, as slowly as possible, to note the drift or observe the waves from a lower altitude.

TAKEOFFS—THE ATTITUDE CHANGES

Trim, pitch angle, and *attitude* are not quite synonymous. In marine parlance, the "trim" of a small boat, say an outboard, refers to the angle at which it floats or runs, usually nose up when planing. In airplanes, this is called the "pitch angle" or "attitude." The "trim" of an airplane usually refers to the stabilizer setting at which it flies hands off or to the residual nose or tail heaviness if it is out of trim. The nose up or nose down *angle* is the "pitch angle" or "attitude."

The attitude of taxiing landplanes is fixed by the landing gear up to the point of rotation for takeoff. The attitude of taxiing seaplanes changes with the speed. The displacement, or at-rest attitude, is slightly nose up when the center of buoyancy is directly under the center of gravity. The aircraft is then floating on its normal waterline. The attitude will remain practically unchanged until full power is applied to climb onto the step. Then the nose is pulled as high as possible with full up-elevator. When the seaplane is planing and taxiing at a high speed, the attitude should be held with moderate up-elevator approximately at the waterline angle. A few high-powered seaplanes will attain planing speed even without help from up-elevator, but they will oscillate and throw much more spray.

Figure 2 shows the relationship of these several attitudes or trim angles. The attitudes are best visualized by holding the edge of a sheet of paper on the angle under consideration. This becomes the water surface, and the seaplane will look quite realistic in its several attitudes during takeoff. Placing the edge of the paper above the angle lines will reveal the amount of hull under water and provide an understanding of the water forces at work in each phase of takeoff.

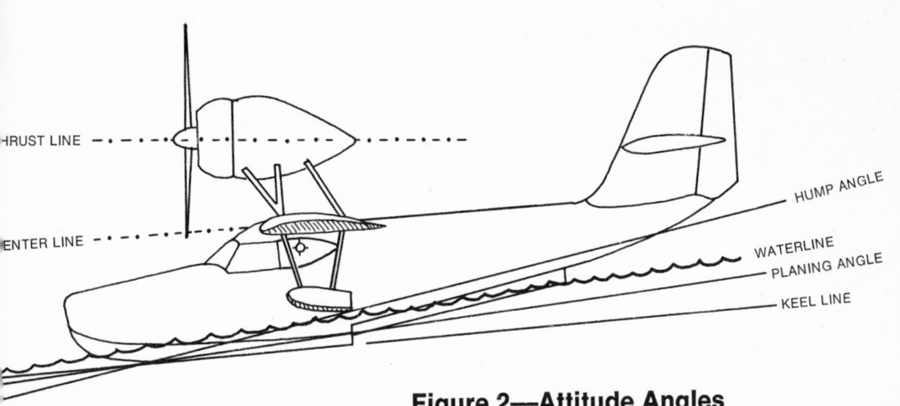

Figure 2—Attitude Angles

Without up-elevator the drag on the bottom acting below the C.G., or center of gravity, causes her to plane in a slight nose-down attitude, and she might never take off by herself. However, on a rippled sea, most seaplanes can be trimmed slightly nose-up and will take themselves off even with free controls, but then will have to be quickly retrimmed to prevent an overly steep climb. If they are normally trimmed and allowed to accelerate hands off, most seaplanes, floats or boats, will *porpoise* (see Chapter 6, p.55).

Figure 3 will help to elaborate the following discussion. Both thrust and drag forces vary during takeoff. On a landplane, the engine thrust has to overcome only the rolling

Figure 3—Water Drag at Takeoff

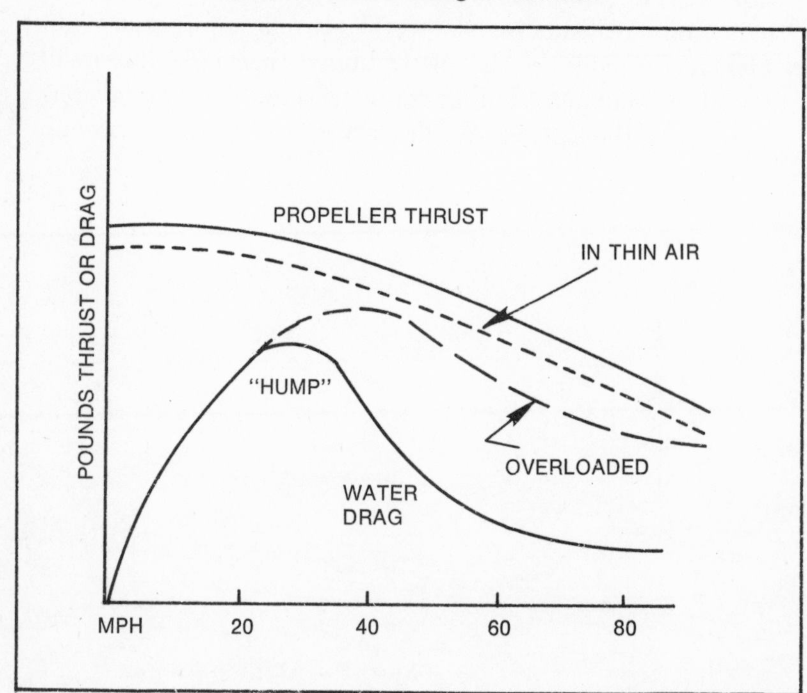

friction of the wheels and the steadily increasing air drag. On a seaplane, the water drag becomes a major part of the forces resisting acceleration. It peaks rapidly at somewhere around 20 to 25 mph as the hull is driven up onto its step and into a planing attitude. This point is called the "hump," both because there is a hump in the resistance curve and because the aircraft actually feels as if it had passed over a hump. After this point, the hull is on the step and water resistance decreases.

The resistance or drag at the hump is greatly increased by overloading, by thin air (either very hot climate or high altitude)—and by glassy water conditions. Then no little "lubricating" air bubbles slide under the hull, as they do when small choppy waves exist. If the drag exceeds the thrust, there is no further acceleration. The aircraft won't take off. But if the pilot is just able to squeeze through this point, he will probably be able to complete the takeoff, although it will be a long one. During the last part of the run, water drag acting backwards on the hull bottom and thrust acting high up at the propeller will necessitate a light up-elevator pull for the plane to become airborne. The solid curves in the diagram are for normal conditions. The broken line shows the effect of overloading. The dotted line shows the reduction of thrust in thin air. There may be another no-go point, particularly on glassy water, just before the takeoff speed can be attained.

In order to keep the best trim angle for takeoff firmly in mind, the following practice procedure is recommended. After passing through the hump and getting on the step, throttle back the engine to 60 to 65 percent power for the rest of the takeoff. There is an optimum angle for best takeoff, and at this power setting the aircraft is very sensitive. If the nose is too high, water resistance on the hull will prevent a gain in speed and may even slow the aircraft down. Likewise, if the nose is too low, the water resistance will be increased because more wetted area is in the water. The "feel" of the aircraft for best trim can be learned very quickly in this manner, and it is valuable as a refresher after a period of inactivity in water operations. Of course, final takeoff under these conditions will be longer than usual, and a clear water path of two or three miles should be selected. For this exercise waves should be relatively low.

During the entire takeoff run in a flying boat, aileron control is required much more than on a landplane or twin-float seaplane. The flying boat is supported only on one central hull once the hump speed is passed. The torque effect of the propeller becomes much more noticeable when there is no lateral support from spread-apart wheels or floats.

The spray pattern must also be considered in water takeoffs. As the craft accelerates, an increasing spray blister is thrown outward from the bow or bows. The heaviest spray occurs right at the hump. The point at which the blister, or fan, leaves the chines moves rapidly aft as the ship goes through the hump and onto the step. The period during which spray pours through the propeller disc must be reduced to a minimum to prevent pitting of metal propeller blades. Even if it misses them in smooth water, it will still pour into them in rough water.

The amount of water beating depends on the propeller location. On twin-float, single-engine seaplanes, it becomes momentarily doubly heavy when the inside blisters from the two floats combine. Fortunately, these props are far enough forward for the spray to pass underneath early in the takeoff. The props on twin-engine floatplanes are directly over the float and almost perfectly protected, except in rough water when spray flies all over the place anyway. The prop location on single-engine tractor flying boats is also protected.

On single-engine pushers, where the prop is farther aft, it is protected by the hull underneath, except that all the spray originates forward of the prop, and plenty will always be flying around at the trailing edge of the wing. If the wing sprouts from the deck of the hull, it will partially shield the prop. The props of twin- or multi-engine flying boats plunge deeply into the blisters until they pass aft. Regardless of the configuration, help the props all you can.

TORQUE EFFECTS

Single-engine airplanes, when climbing at full power, often require right rudder to hold the heading. This is incorrectly called *torque*. More accurately, it is torque *effect*. A tractor propeller turning clockwise, as viewed from the pilot's seat, exerts a *twisting reaction* on the crank shaft that tends to roll the airplane to the left. That truly is torque. When resisted by the lift forces spread over a wide wingspan, torque is negligible. It becomes noticeable only on very high-powered fighters with large-geared props. The rudder force carried in climb is required to offset the "race rotation," which means the twisting motion within the slipstream as it flows back over the tail. It strikes the fin from the port side, and therefore most fins are offset to port to alleviate this force. Race rotation adds a downward force on the starboard stabilizer, upward on the port. Thus, this portion of the race rotation wants to roll the airplane to the right. The stabilizer span is so short that this effect cannot be measured.

Rolling forces from torque during the takeoff run are absorbed by the rolling wheels and are not noticed on land. Nor are they felt on twin-float seaplanes. Flying boats, on the other hand, are free to roll about their one keel—and they do. During a straight-line takeoff, the port wing-tip float bears on the water and usually cannot be lifted by the aileron until enough airflow is established. On calm days, if the pilot insists on a straight course, there may be an appreciable heel to port as the hull rises onto the step. If this is annoying, you can use centrifugal force to level the wings by starting the takeoff run a little to starboard of your desired course, then turning into it. Of course, if you have a "left-hand" turning propeller, torque forces are reversed. Also, on pusher flying boats with the propeller behind the engine, it is seen from the tail as a left-hand turning propeller with torque forces also reversed. Don't be distressed about a wing-tip float planing on the water. As long as it is planing, the rearward drag forces are slight. Even when it is fully submerged, the lift force exceeds the drag.

5

TAXIING

STEP TAXIING

Taxiing on the step at two-thirds power with speeds between the hump and takeoff is safe, useful, and a lot of fun. Use full power only long enough to get on the step, then throttle back to continue at minimum planing speed with relatively little noise, extremely important if you wish to continue operating in those waters. Don't taxi toward boats at high speed even if you have ample control to steer with great accuracy—it scares them! Remember, you look pretty big and awful fast. They will like you more when you taxi fast away from them. The rules of navigation and courtesy apply to all water maneuvers. An aircraft on the water is a boat sharing the facilities of harbors and lakes with all other boats. Taxiing patterns must be planned with consideration for all others.

Outbound step taxiing is useful to get far away from a crowded harbor before making the roar of a takeoff. Inbound, landings can be made well "outside" and then you can purr fast and accurately into the mouth of a channel before dropping off the step. Landplane pilots are amazed at the relative tightness of acceptable turns. Flying boats can be banked with ailerons when on the step. When the inside tip float is just flicking the tops of the waves and the hull is riding high, the bank angle produces enough inward force on the bottom and wings to permit tighter and more comfortable turns than twin-float planes. As the turn tightens, more power will be needed to maintain a little more than hump speed. Boats, particularly twin-engine, can make extremely sharp turns when added power keeps them nose up and just not quite sinking off the step. The turn requires about half power, and the noise is within generally accepted limits outside the mooring area of a harbor.

TAXIING AND SAILING—ALL ADRIFT

Do you remember how baffled, confused, and discouraged you were about three instruction hours before your first solo? You'll get that feeling again when you undertake taxiing under difficult wind conditions. But I promise, you will eventually understand. Mastery and skill will soon follow. The problems are not those of flight but rather of seamanship. Nevertheless, a good seaman who is not an air pilot will be more confounded than a pilot who is not yet a seaman. So take heart; yours is the better approach. Normally, you will work up gradually to operations in ever windier days. To understand the whole operation, let us first consider taxiing in *very high wind.*

Understanding will come after listing the applicable forces, controls, and complexities between them. To simplify discussion, twin-engine thrusts and reversible propellers will be postponed. Don't quail at the following pattern. Read it fast, be humbly impressed, then refer back to it as the discussion develops.

FORCES AT WORK

Thrust —Acts only forward.
Drag —Acts backward on movement through water.
—Acts sideways to backwards from wind.
Wind —By its strength.
—By its direction.
Current —By strength.
—By direction.
Water Resistance—To sideways motion or "keel effect."

CONTROLS—AVAILABLE

Power—By thrust.
Drag —By wheels down, if amphib.
—By flaps down.
—By opening doors on light floatplanes.
Yaw —By water rudders.
—By air rudder when in strong slipstream.
—By ailerons when "sailing."
Roll —By ailerons, only on boats.
Attitude—By elevator.
—More by speed through the water.
Centrifugal—Outward in turns.

COMPLEXITIES

Thrust —Increases yaw—always wanted.
—Adds speed—seldom wanted.
Wind —Strongly affects turn.
—Different for low or high speeds.
—Causes unwanted roll.
Centrifugal —Starts only above moderate speed.
Sideward water and air resistances
—Beneficial in "sailing."
—Overturning in crosswinds.

Unsymmetrical drag—If the downwind float of a floatplane is nearly buried, it produces more drag than its twin. The effect is more pronounced from a buried float on a flying boat, but these forces are usually overridden by others and will be ignored.

TURNS OUT OF THE WIND

With no control forces applied, every idling seaplane will weathercock into the wind. There she wants to stay. To turn out of a strong wind, it helps to understand the effect of keel plane area. If the craft is in a normal displacement attitude, the center of resistance to lateral motion through the water is ahead of the centers of buoyancy and gravity. That is, the lesser keel plane area aft allows the tail to slither sideways and weathercock. If a sudden blast of power is applied with full up-elevator, the attitude rears up to a nose-high position with the aft part of the keel deeply submerged, causing more keel area aft than forward. She may even weathercock out of the wind and help to make a downwind turn. In any case, she will respond nicely to the rudder because the slipstream blast has brought it to life. A further help is the centrifugal force which, acting outward on the turn, tends to cancel the heeling effect of the wind.

But don't linger! You are in the dilemma of needing power for control when increasing speed is a detriment. Now is the time to cope and cooperate by applying turning inertia. If you have elected a turn to starboard, give it up and give the ship her will. Change as fast as possible to a port turn. She will weathercock with alacrity and be swinging fast as she passes again through the eye of the wind. Retain this inertia and keep her coming. She will complete the whole 270-

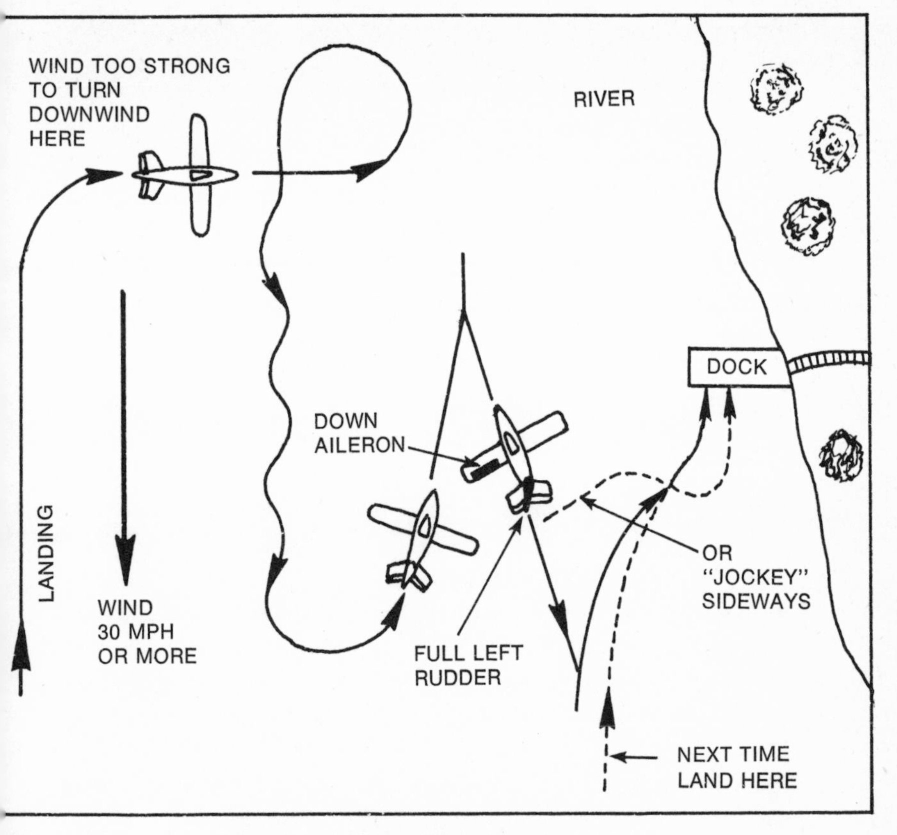

Figure 4—High Wind Taxiing

degree turn to port with ease and attain the desired downwind course (figure 4).

DOWNWIND TAXIING

Now, with the wind pushing from behind, the problem is to go as slowly as possible while retaining steering control. When she veers, correct instantly with a very sharp momentary throttle blast. At the end of the downwind stretch you will wish to turn back into the wind, but the ship will want to much more than you! She will turn fast; the centrifugal force will now add to the wind's force. A capsize is imminent, particularly in floatplanes that present a high side area to the wind. When it is time to turn, and she is straight downwind, as slow as you can make it, just slightly reverse the air rudder or steer with the water rudder to start the turn. She'll do the rest. Down-aileron on the outside wing will help prevent excessive heel, but only after the midpoint is reached.

Both floatplanes and boats will heel alarmingly. The flying boat is generally more secure, because it is closer to the water and the wind does not get under the upwind wing as strongly. Further, the long moment arm of the wing-tip float tends to reduce really dangerous heel. The float may be crowded under water quite early in the turn when the lifting force on its bottom is overwhelmed. However, usually when the water flows over the cambered deck of the float more lift is added and the turn is completed with no further heel, the float running submerged with the waterline halfway up the float struts. If a floatplane heels so far that a wing tip gets in the water, all is lost. If a wing tip of a boat gets in the water the rearward force turns her back downwind. The increased drag stops her dead in the water and she weathercocks around the other way with no forward speed. This is not recommended!

CROSSWIND TAXIING

But suppose we wanted to taxi 90 degrees crosswind under these rugged conditions? We will find, as the Maine man said, "You can't get there from here," at least by normal methods. We have turned directly crosswind; we are heeling severely; to hold the desired course we add more power, and we go faster and faster in a huge cloud of flying spray. We have to give up. Now is the time to learn sailing.

SAILING

If we can't conquer the wind forces, let them work for us. Allow her to weathercock into the wind and remain idling, and she'll pick up a fair speed straight backward. Now we can elect a downwind course, to a certain extent, by using keel effect to sail sideways and backwards. Head her out of the wind, stay to port, as far as she will go by turning the rudder to port. The air rudder will swing her to port, but the ported water rudder will be nearly ineffectual. However, since the hull is moving aft, the water rudder turned to starboard may be more effective than the air rudder. If so, use it so. If not, retract it and use port rudder. To gain a little more, use aileron drag. The down-aileron offers more drag than the up-aileron, so roll the ship to starboard and the heading will swing still more to port. It is helped by the forward acting drag of the starboard wing-tip float.

Looking aft, you will observe that the side forces on the yawed floats or hull are heading her astern perhaps as much as 30 degrees away from the wind direction. Since the water is also escaping under the floats to some extent, there is a little "leeway," and the actual course made good may be some 20 to 25 degrees out of the wind, crabbing to starboard as you drift aft.

At any time, you can taxi upwind about 30 degrees to starboard simply by adding enough power and steering with both rudders. Thus, you can "tack" backward and forward, using sideways movement to ultimately reach your objective.

A further refinement in sailing is to add just enough engine power to hold the boat from moving either up- or downwind, but keep her yawed to starboard. The hull or float produces no side force, but the wind blowing over the yawed fuselage pushes her to starboard. She will then slowly move in a direction at right angles to the wind. Should you add thrust, she would move steadily a little upwind, say to the northeast; use a little less thrust, and she will take a course to the southeast. Here the low hull of a flying boat offers less "sail area" than the high fuselage of a floatplane. Whether it is faster to reach your objective by zigzag 30-degree tacks, or by sailing at 90 degrees, depends on the aircraft, the conditions, the pilot, and the impatience of the passengers. With a little practice, you can jockey her where you wish, and soon you will no longer feel "all adrift" but will be able to master pretty foul operating conditions.

So far we have assumed no reversible propeller, no wheels to lower for added drag, and no twin-engine thrust for steering, all of which are great advantages. A reversible prop can stop the boat dead in the water after you have taxied downwind before attempting the critical upwind turn. Dragging wheels going downwind can be a major help, but they had better be raised when you want to swing fast around upwind. Two engines permit steering with power. They are better than the rudder in preventing excessive swerving downwind, particularly in conjunction with wheel drag. The upwind turn is pleasingly snappy. Twin-engine straight crosswind taxiing with wheels down is accomplished in higher wind with even more spray—if you are willing to accept severe prop erosion. But for short periods, it permits getting in between wharfs, for example, with real assurance.

With two reversible propellers you can master almost all conditions. Unfortunately, these props appear mostly on larger amphibians which move with disconcerting momentum in tight places, scaring you out of using the fine control they provide, unless the wind is very calm. There was a period when "Albatrosses" were used to retrieve dummy sonar buoys from the water after drop-release tests. Using the props for both speed and directional control, we would jockey until the floating buoy was between the port wing-tip float and the hull, and then, by reversing the starboard prop, swing the hull so that the door aft of the wing was positioned to enable us to lift out the buoy by hand without even using a boat hook. If sea conditions are smooth enough to permit, it is possible for air-sea-rescue "Albatrosses" to pick downed pilots out of liferafts this way, but extreme care must be used not to let the raft get anywhere near the turning prop. If the man in the raft is not incapacitated, a heaving line is usually thrown to him for safety; otherwise, an inflatable dinghy is used.

So much for extremely high winds. They are infrequent and marginal. This discussion described technique useful in merely fresh winds and delineated the limits.

CROSSWIND TECHNIQUE

Crosswind landings and takeoffs are much easier on water than land. This is due to the easier, less tense psychology of the pilot, perhaps because he knows the water is a yielding and moderately excusing surface. No hull keel really likes to skid sideways through the water; it is there to prevent sideways motion. But a slight skid creates much less side force than rubber tires on concrete. Today, landplanes always land on runways and therefore are more or less crosswind on almost every landing. On a two-runway airport, this is so on all but four headings out of 360 degrees! Seaplanes often operate from canals and narrow rivers, but usually they can opt for a true upwind landing. If they cannot, there is no great problem either.

Let us first review landplane crosswind techniques. (Quite likely you will wish to modify them after you have had crosswind experience on the water!) The approach course is always straight and in line with the runway, and the landing run is always envisioned as straight down the center line. Let us assume the wind is from the left. If nothing is done, the airplane will be drifting to the right at touchdown, and there will be a major jerk from the side load on the tires when they meet the runway. An erratic rollout follows, if not a full ground loop.

One method of eliminating side load at touchdown is to lower the upwind wing while holding both heading and course, resulting in a steady sideslip, enough to offset the drift to the right. The low wing is rolled up to level just before touchdown, late enough to prevent generating buildup of side drift to the right.

The other method is to hold wings level and crab the approach by heading enough upwind to hold the course. Sharp right rudder straightens the heading just before touchdown enough to oppose side drift to the right.

Both of these methods require keen judgment in timing and instant skillful control. Inexperienced passengers dislike both methods. Worse, neither answers the big problem of how to cancel the crosswind force during rollout. If the airplane is a tail-dragger—that is, one with a tail wheel—the right brake must be used enough to prevent an upwind ground loop. (In the old days, without brakes, the airplane almost always ground looped. The only solution was an airport with three or more intersecting runways, or else we didn't fly that day!) If the airplane has a modern tricycle gear, the scuffing forces will try to head it downwind to the right, and the left brake must be applied. In either case, the ball moves out of the center bars measuring the amount of side force being resisted—and your passengers dislike that feeling more.

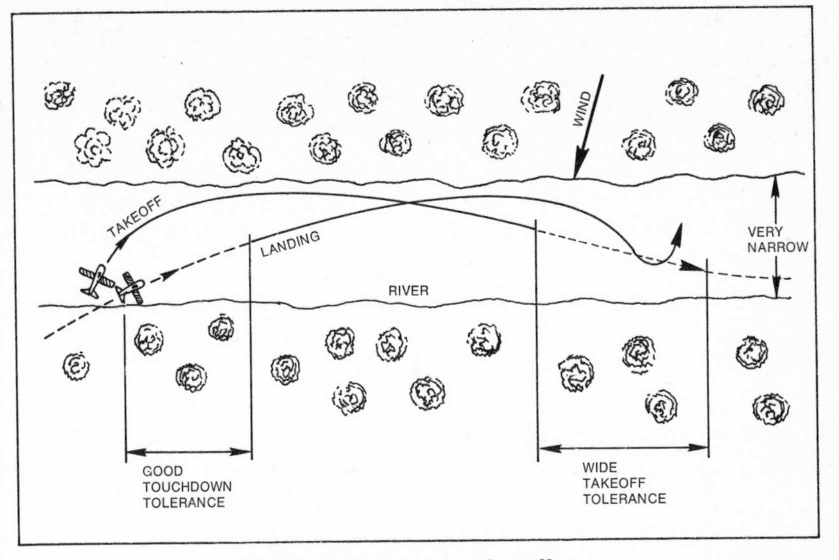

Figure 5—Crosswind Landing

The seaplane pilot instinctively uses the downwind-arc method of crosswind landing, so named by an unknown Navy pilot and Leighton Collins, in a long discussion in the magazine, *Air Facts*. In figure 5, the pilot approaches his intended landing spot with neither slip nor skid by heading enough upwind so that a gentle curve in the last stage of approach will reach the touchdown point with no drift. Not being confined to a runway ahead, he takes full advantage of familiar centrifugal force and turns gently downwind just enough to throw it against the side force of the wind to exactly cancel out that force. The ball stays precisely in the middle. The runout is a gentle curve of *decreasing* radius, because more curvature is needed to create the desired centrifugal force as the speed becomes slower. No alert, sensitive judgment or skill is needed, because only slight corrections can be continuously applied. The approach course is not held rigidly to a straight line. The touchdown point may be early or quite late, as the diagram indicates. The rollout curve is gently adjusted as required when it occurs, mostly by the feel of the seat of your pants that is always the basic clue to accurate flying. There are no straining forces anywhere in the airplane structure. The slightly curving approach raises the upwind wing so slightly it is not alarming. It *feels* right even if at first it doesn't look quite right.

Use the same principles for crosswind water takeoffs. The airplane is headed between the wind and the necessary takeoff direction. This is not an exact judgment. It can be readily adjusted as soon as she accelerates and you get the feel. The takeoff curve is gentle, with *increasing* radius. All the easy tolerances again apply. The point of liftoff is not sensitive. She will come off when she is ready. It will *feel* right.

If you now look back and observe the wake in either operation, you will be astonished at how little these curved paths deviate from a straight line. The width between the point of maximum belly and a line connecting the beginning and end of the run is surprisingly small. You should now try it out in a narrow river section, slanting in over the downwind bank, as shown in figure 5. When taking off, start as near the downwind bank as water depth permits and elect a curved course tangent to the upwind bank. As you then arc slightly downwind, you will find the increasing speed permits wide variance in the final part of the run. Try out the method in narrower and narrower sections of a river. Your confidence and skill will increase rapidly.

Try it on a runway the next time you fly a landplane. Strange as it seems, a 100-foot-wide runway is enough to accept downwind arcs in extremely strong crosswinds, even for the 10,000-pound airplanes, landing fast and taking a relatively long rollout. It is equally good for a 20,000-pound airplane on a 200-foot-wide runway. The tower operators may be surprised at the off-center-line approach, but the resulting smooth, unwobbly runout will convince them.

6

PORPOISING AND SKIPPING

Seawater is yielding, but it is also heavy, about eight hundred times as heavy as air. When it flows under or around a hull, it can exert great forces that increase as the square of the speed. It is not surprising that forces from a water surface are more complex than those from smooth land. Wheel forces act only at a fixed point along a fuselage. Water forces act along a hull at a constantly changing center of pressure depending on pitch, wave action, and the dynamic hull motions. Hull bottom lines have been refined through years of testing and experience to produce the required lift forces for takeoff and landing. They provide maximum lift and minimum drag. More important, they reduce changes in the location of the center of lift to the minimum. However, some complexity still remains, resulting in the minor problems of porpoising and skipping.

PORPOISING

Porpoising is a rhythmic pitching motion, nose up and nose down, that may occur on takeoff and landing. It is a dynamic instability that the pilot damps out with elevator control. The type of water surface most conducive to porpoising is a dead calm sea in no wind, though any uniform wave system may aggravate the motion. If the pitch angle is held too low, the lifting forces at the bow increase. If the pitch is too high, the repelling forces near the after step increase. Therefore, when an oscillation is once established, it may tend to increase. The motion is harder to check on larger flying boats because increased pitching inertia induces such oscillation to depress the bow, then stern, more deeply.

So also the pilot may induce or amplify the motion by Pilot Induced Oscillations, or PIO, a term well known to test pilots and manifest in other phases of flight. When a pilot perceives a repeating oscillation and attempts to control against it, there is a lag in his perception and his muscular movement of the controls. The mental process of observing the need and analyzing the corrective action, plus his slight delay in applying force to the controls, and in the correct amount, requires an appreciable interval. If there is any additional flexibility in the airplane control system, the final corrective movement may arrive at the tail after the oscillation has started to reverse. So he reverses his correction. Again it arrives late. He is amplifying the oscillations and they further increase. That is PIO.

All this sounds pretty serious—but it isn't. It is presented in detail to explain a puzzling seaplane behavior. When an experienced pilot senses the approach of porpoising, he restrains the control and holds the pitch in the correct trim for that part of the takeoff run.

Figure 6 explains these effects. Porpoising will not occur if the pitch angle is held correctly within tolerant limits or returned immediately after divergence perhaps caused by a swell. If the pilot holds up-elevator too long after the hump, he may carry into the upper porpoising limit, as shown by

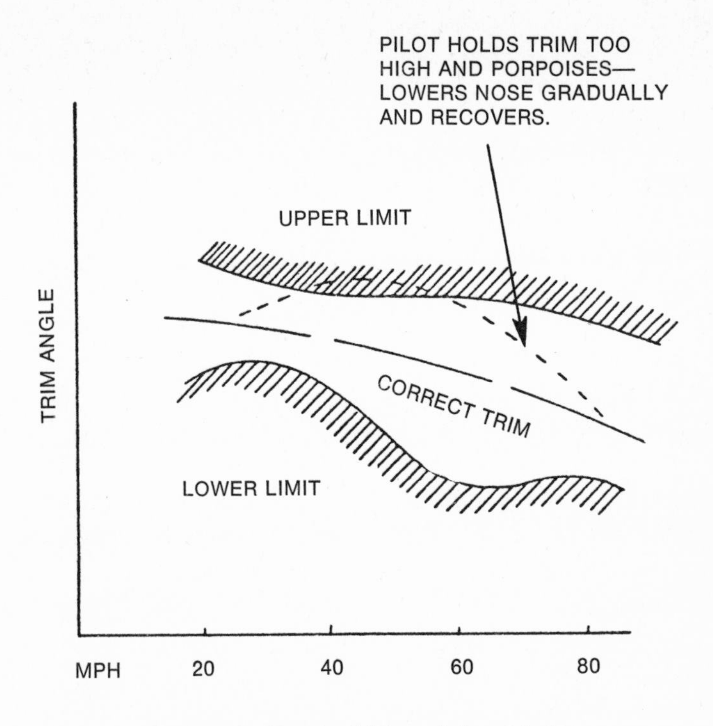

Figure 6—Typical Porpoising Limits

the dotted line. Or if he pushes the seaplane over onto the step too sharply, he can enter the lower range. Porpoising does not start until a degree or two after the aircraft has entered the critical range; on the other hand, it does not *stop* until a degree or two after the aircraft has passed *out* of the range. Porpoising continues when the corrective action lags so much the opposite limit is penetrated. PIO has occurred.

Note that the limits diverge after passing the hump, but converge during a landing when decelerating from right to left in the diagram. Many seaplanes make one or two innocuous porpoises as they settle off the step. The rapidity of the oscillations is inversely proportional to the size of the airplane, and although it is less likely to occur in small seaplanes, they require faster corrective action than large ones.

The upper and lower limits are as wide apart as the designer could make them and are specific for each seaplane. However, changes in loading and flap angle will modify the limits. Increase in gross weight raises the lower limit considerably, the upper limit less so. The tolerance is reduced at hump and takeoff speed. Operations from high-altitude lakes are the equivalent of increasing the gross. A forward center of gravity location raises the lower limit at hump and high speed; an aft location decreases the possibility of high-angle porpoising, especially on landing. Flap angle has an important effect. It trims the seaplane toward the lower limit at low speed and may lower the upper limit at high speed. See pages 59-62 for a full discussion of the use of flaps.

Porpoising is not dangerous unless it gets into phase with a swell pattern. Then it may become violent. If so—abandon. If it occurs during takeoff, cut the power and start another run at a different angle to the swell, thus changing the frequency of meeting the swells. If it occurs during landing, pour on the power, take off, and make a new approach on a new course. Experience may be attained under less severe conditions by partial-power step taxiing and deliberately induced porpoising.

SKIPPING—AN ANNOYANCE

Skipping is also an up-and-down motion, but more in "heave" than pitch. Heave refers to the vertical motion of the whole hull up and down without change in the pitch angle. The afterbody behind the step will suddenly suck down, often jumping the plane clear of the water below flying speed. Then there may be several rhythmic skips in a row. It can be further identified by a sharp "snatch" caused by the sudden increase in drag not associated with porpoising.

Skipping usually occurs when landing on smooth water with a relatively high nose-up pitch angle. It happens when the afterbody, which was planing on a small wetted area at the rear step, is suddenly and completely washed by solid green water so that the whole afterbody is wetted. It is a function of hull design or, again, overloading. Under normal load, and with no large waves, the purpose of the main step is to "ventilate" the afterbody so that air is introduced at the sides, thus giving it a chance to plane as the forebody is doing. The skip occurs when this air is cut off. In rough water the afterbody can be smothered by a large wave, momentarily occluding the sides of the step. Since a wave crest is always followed by a trough, this condition is immediately self-correcting. (This phenomenon is discussed in more detail in Chapter 17.)

FLAPS AND ATTITUDE—KEEP THE NOSE UP

When you skiers are charging down a rough hill and are occasionally jumping over hummocks, would you ever dare land in deep snow with the nose of the skis down? Don't ever do it on water either. Water just doesn't like to run uphill. In fact, it won't. When a seaplane touches the water with the nose so low that the keel line rises behind it, the water clinging to the bottom does run "uphill" in relation to the hull. Something has to give. It's the hull that yields. That is, it heaves down rather than lifting the water up. The forebody is sucked down, violently but momentarily. The up forces acting at the curved-up bow are intensified. The increased displacement adds lift. Both these up forces are well ahead of the center of gravity. The hull screams for relief and gets it by suddenly pitching up—violently.

Since the plane could not have touched nose down unless it was flying fast, it surges up in an alarmingly steep climb. Unless full power is added and the wheel is shoved ahead quickly to resume flight, a stall and a crash will follow. A squadron of Air Force pilots assigned to flying boats during the war cracked up five before they learned. They reported, "No matter how fast we came in and held them down on the water, they went out of control even with full flaps!"

The use of full trailing edge flaps is desirable in order to land at minimum speed. But for any given approach speed, the ship flies more nose-down. In a full-flap landing the touchdown occurs with the nose depressed more than during a no-flap landing. When flaps are not used, the landing is faster but more nose-up.

The philosophy of good hull design requires that all water flowing under the bottom must be deflected downward to provide hull lift at any water speed. If you will raise a flying boat model above your eyes and look down the bottom, as the water surface sees the approaching hull, you will observe how the bottom lines accomplish this purpose. If you tilt it until the bow hides the step, the reason for the sudden suck-down becomes clear.

The pitch angle of a tail-dragger landplane can be trimmed by the pilot during takeoff. Although most of the takeoff run of a tricycle-geared landplane is determined by the landing gear, the pilot increases the angle for lift-off, or "rotates." The best pitch angle for seaplanes, however, is determined less by the wing incidence than the optimum for the hull. Therefore, wings are attached to the hull of a boat with a greater angle of incidence measured to the hull center line. It is often 5 degrees. Also, the keel of many boats is at a negative angle to the center line so that the sum of this angle and the incidence is optimum for liftoff—at least 5 degrees.

If this is the case, you may ask, how does it work out when converting landplanes to floatplanes? In that case, the floats are attached with a very large negative angle, perhaps 5 degrees. In flight they are nose down to the airstream and offer unfortunate drag.

For the flying boat with which the Air Force squadron had the trouble, the angles in relation to the center line of the hull were: Incidence— +3°; Keel line— —2°. The angles at which the keel touched the water for different speeds and flap settings were:

Touchdown speed, mph	0° *Flaps*	30° *Flaps*	60° *Flaps*
70	—	9.9°	7.3°
80	9.9	5.3	2.7
90	6.6	2.1	— .2
100	4.2	— .1	—2.6

The speed at which the plane bounced off the water with full flaps was slightly above 90 mph. The table shows the tolerance at touchdown even with full flaps was 7 degrees or 20 mph. So don't worry. All this discussion is by way of explanation. Modern high-lift devices on the leading edge, such as slats or Kreuger flaps, bring the center of lift farther forward on the wing chord. Had they been used then, the nose-down attitude would have been reduced.

An experienced seaplane pilot uses his flaps somewhat differently than he would on a landplane. Under normal conditions he will use half-flap for landings because it reduces speed nearly to minimum while retaining a good nose-up tolerance for faster-than-normal landings. On very rough water, he will use full flaps because they assure absolute minimum landing speed to reduce wave pounding, and because the impacts are heavier when the hull strikes the waves nose up. Bouncing off the waves is reduced when the hull attitude is more nearly level.

Unlike landplanes taking off from runways, seaplanes usually have ample emergency landing space ahead. Getting airborne early and out of debris is important. Half-flap take-offs are more common because it is less important for a twin-engine boat to attain speed and altitude, permitting continued flight on one engine. Even if full flaps might get the seaplane airborne a little earlier, they should not be used.

I found this out during a rough-water takeoff in a seaway dotted with four-foot pulp logs. A comber bounced us into the air a bit early, and I used nearly full up-elevator to hold us there. The wing didn't quite stall, but as we climbed out of the ground (water) cushion, the angle of downwash over the tail increased. The tail stalled. We dropped back the ten feet or so onto the water, the ship nosing herself down enough to cleave two more wave crests rather gently. By then our speed had increased enough to permit a normal climb out. Naturally, I figured this all out after the event! If I had used 30 degrees flap, the total takeoff distance would have been less.

7

SEAMANSHIP

The term "seamanship" applies to the judgment and skill a captain uses in maneuvering his boat under all conditions. It is a balance between securing maximum utility and preventing damage to his and other craft.

There is little hazard in any water maneuvers with a seaplane, with one great exception. Always keep in mind that a turning propeller is a disc of certain death. Your passengers may help in anchoring, mooring, and docking. It is your responsibility to instruct and caution them and to monitor their every movement outside the cabin while the engine is running. This need not be alarming. On a two-way road, when we step out of a car or pass another coming from the opposite direction, instant death is there too, only a few feet away. On the road you are subject to your and others' carelessness. In a seaplane your own carelessness is the only threat.

Easy does it in close quarters. Make no sudden moves. Go as slowly as possible. Engine idling speed should be adjusted in advance to be as slow as possible. If the engine has six or more cylinders and a metal prop, it has enough inertia to permit "blipping" the throttle to go even slower.

Switch off, then turn on again just before the prop stops turning, a process that will approximately halve forward speed of minimum idle. If the engine has been idling for a period before cutoff, it will usually quit smoothly without kicking over and be ready for a prompt start if needed. But if you approach a boat, mooring, or dock too fast, cut it with the mixture control so the prop is absolutely dead by the time people start fending off. Amphibian landing gears should be down and dragging. As soon as possible after landing, request and use local knowledge on harbor and lake conditions and facilities.

ANCHORING

An anchor is a mudhook. It doesn't hold a plane down to the bottom. It hooks into the mud or clay and resists only a tangential pull sideways. For that reason it needs plenty of scope, the extra length of anchor line permitting it to pull sideways on the bottom, not up. The minimum scope for most conditions is seven times the water depth. I usually use more.

HOLDING GROUND

Holding ground describes the type of bottom that will assure a good anchor "bite." The anchor bites best in clay, followed by fine gravel, then sticky mud, finally sand. Anchors will slide over rocky bottom unless by chance a fluke catches under a large rock. Even then it may twist out from under when the wind changes the angle of pull. You can test the set of the anchor in the bottom by sudden yanks on the line to see if it is holding. Try not to anchor in water more than 20 feet deep unless you have a very long anchor line. When you come into a strange harbor, river, or lake there is usually a cluster of moored or anchored boats where the best shelter, depth, and holding ground exist. You should anchor close to the edge of the cluster, leaving enough distance from adjacent boats to allow you to swing free as the wind changes and have start-up taxiing clearance in any wind upon departure.

The line is secured to the bow cleat of a boat, and may be secured to one bow cleat on a floatplane for a stop of short duration in light wind. However, if the floatplane is to be left anchored, the line should be secured to the eye of a bridle, or V line, attached to the bows of both floats to insure that the ship holds steady. Before leaving the aircraft, check for a few minutes to see how she is lying to the wind and tide and make sure there is sufficient swinging room.

Before going ashore, take a couple of ranges on shore objects to make sure of the position of the seaplane, and when ashore take another range so that any position shift can be detected in the event the anchor should drag. Average holding ground with the anchor size recommended for your particular seaplane should be adequate for 15- to 18-knot winds, but make extra provision for anchoring overnight. A second and much heavier anchor should be borrowed from shore and dropped from a small boat. Check the weather once or twice during the night, and keep a flashlight and the small boat handy on shore.

For the same total weight, two anchors will hold much more securely than one. Many experienced owners carry a pair. When using both, the second anchor should be dropped with some 50 percent longer line about 30 degrees to one side of the first. If the wind boxes the compass, the short-line anchor may drag in a circle around the other, but both will always be working.

Anchors and handling lines are stored in bow compartments on boats and in one of the float compartments in floatplanes, accessible through hinged hatches. The top of a float affords an excellent handling deck, particularly if there are wing struts to hold on to. It is incumbent on the designer of small flying boats to provide a cabin windshield hatch, a small side stepping deck, or a flat deck under large double-opening hatches, to give the anchor man a safe stance. A grip handle on the center line of the windshield helps no end. On larger flying boats a large bow compartment permits the anchor man to crawl forward under the instrument board and operate through a hatch safely at waist height.

Anchors that have set deeply into the mud may be hard to free, but they yield to a direct upward lift which pries out the flukes. Bring the first of a pair aboard before starting the engine. When the engine is running, the anchor man can lift the remaining anchor as the hull passes over. If it still fails to break out, take a hitch around the cleat, and the inertia of the plane should lift it. If the amphibian landing gear is down, be careful not to foul an anchor line around a wheel or you'll be in a mean mess. On a small seaplane these maneuvers can be done solo if the wind permits.

MOORING

Most small-boat harbors have vacant moorings you can borrow, at least for a short while. If you land frequently in the same harbor or lake, set your own mooring; it's much more convenient and secure than riding to a light anchor. In a hurricane a 100-pound mushroom mooring anchor will hold well, though a 200-pound mushroom is needed for larger seaplanes.

Mooring buoys are low, round metal floats or larger plastic balls. On rugged coasts heavy cedar poles are used, which often project a couple of feet above the water.

This is not so much an economy measure as it is a security one to put a snubber in the chain preventing wave action from snatching. It nearly doubles the holding power. When approaching a mooring, don't forget your propeller discs on single-engine floatplanes or twin-engine boats. Don't over-run any pole or pickup buoy high enough to enter the disc, or get the buoy between the floats where it might batter the spreader struts.

Approach the mooring slowly, directly upwind, and switch off when it is clear that the "carry" of the plane will bring you to it. Or err on the early side, since you can always restart for a moment. Most moorings will have a pennant, or short stout line, you can bring aboard by a boathook. Usually the eye splices will be too large for your small cleat. You can slip it over and keep the eye closed by a couple of hitches at the throat with a handling line. Attach the pennant to a bridle if you have twin floats. Don't be embarrassed if you occasionally miss the buoy the first time. Experienced yachtsmen whose craft have less windage than yours think nothing of it.

When leaving a mooring it is good practice to drop the pennant and pass your handling line through the buoy eye and back to your cleat so it will run free through the eye as you gather speed. If the buoy is low enough to clear all parts of your plane, you can snub the line short and hold until the engine starts. If the buoy is high and you do not wish to take a chance on starting by previously dropping the mooring and drifting back, you can use a long length of handling line so that when the engine starts, you turn away from the buoy promptly, freeing the line and hauling it through the mooring eye as you pass. Make sure the wing-tip float passes over it. On twin-engine boats, avoid getting under way with only one engine running. Start both quickly lest you go in helpless circles while attempting to start the other.

BOARDING A YACHT

Mooring to the stern of an anchored boat or yacht is made the same way, but *never* overrun or come up too fast. Close the final gap by throwing a handling line to the crew on the boat. This is preferable to having them throw a line to the aircraft, because they might heave before the prop is stopped.

Sailboats with deep keels tend to lie to the wind, but motorboats yaw steadily from side to side when the wind blows over 10 knots. You may aim for the stern only to find it is moving away sideways. In that case, throw the line farther or wait for her return. Once aboard, trail your craft off with a very long line, and even then watch out the boats don't yaw in opposite directions, causing a wing tip to get chummy with your guest's yacht. Both craft tend to behave and lie better in winds below 10 knots or over 20.

DOCKING

A wharf is a large structure usually built on piles to accommodate large boats. It may also be called a dock or pier, but usually "dock" refers to a smaller landing facility. A float, sometimes called a raft, is small and rises and falls on the tide. It is held off from a dock by a sloping foot ramp and small anchors. It is inadvisable to attempt to bring a seaplane to a wharf. In lakes, most docks are low to the water, and in the absence of tide, floats are unnecessary. In this discussion, docking refers to making fast at any facility low enough to accommodate small boats.

We have already discussed taxiing technique to reach a dock. Now we are interested in how to come alongside and secure. If the wind is much over six knots, don't approach a downwind dock without a helper to receive you. It is easy to make a cautious approach to an up-current dock, but hazardous if the current is setting you toward the dock. The wing of either a floatplane or a flying boat will project over the dock, so make sure in your selection that piles and the foot ramp are lower than wing height. Many floatplane pilots favor high wings over low because they clear higher objects, but most small-boat docks are quite acceptable to either.

Frequently, you can bring a floatplane neatly alongside, like any boat. If conditions require you to approach at any angle, nose the lead float in gently and secure at both bows, or by bow and stern lines with one float alongside. A flying boat approaches slowly, either nose on or at an angle, in which case the man on the dock catches the wing tip, allowing the bow to swing in for a two-point docking.

In laying to a dock, let the aircraft trail off downwind on a single line if wind direction permits, but keep a watch for changes. Or tie the nose short and rest a wing-tip pontoon on the float. Even better, if the float is narrow enough, lift the wing right over and float it on the other side, then tie the hull alongside with bow and stern lines. Most any suitable dock will be rimmed with a bumper; otherwise, use a life preserver as a fender at a point contact. Always leave someone to keep watch, unless it is dead calm and likely to remain so. Leaving a dock is no problem unless the wind or current is then dead on it. If so, accept a small-boat tow into a clear area before starting the engine.

TOWING

When any flying boat is towed by the bow it will wallow and yaw violently from side to side, which is acceptable only for a short tow. If a long tow is needed, it pays to rig a bridle from the wing fittings above the tip floats. Use a long one to reduce inward pull. On twin-engine boats, the bridle should be secured to the prop hubs.

SMALL BOATS

Young teenagers in small outboards love to cluster around moored flying boats waiting the privilege of taking you ashore. Stand ready to direct, and caution them not to barge into your delicate craft. When they come alongside the hull of a flying boat or a low-wing floatplane there may be little clearance under the wing; watch out that the wake of a passing boat doesn't close this clearance with a crunch.

A great many seaplane owners have become a bit soured on water flying because they never learned and practiced these simple rules of seamanship. Try them out yourself, gain confidence, and win that wonderful feeling of flying freedom to, well, most anywhere. And don't forget, a clove hitch, a bowline, and a square knot! (See figure 1, p.29.)

RAMPS

The curved bows of keels are strong enough to contact a sloping ramp at two or three knots without damage. Usually, they will ride up a little, permitting you to debark and get a handling dolly. Light seaplanes are often taxied up a wet wooden ramp on their keels, usually with a guide man at the wing tip to prevent a sudden yaw if one keel stops sliding. Ramps are expensive, but they are usually built out into the water far enough for the lip to be below "low mean water." "Mean" means average, and the seaward end of many ramps terminates in mud flats at extreme low tides. Not infrequently, approaching seaplanes have to use a lot of power as they enter shallow water, only to find that they suddenly leap ahead when the keels actually lift on the slippery mud flats. The resulting banana-peel slide may damage the bow if the throttle is not closed abruptly.

Approach ramps nearly head on. Observation of the wind and tide and the application of common sense will bring success. If a strong wind is blowing across the ramp, approach upwind and make a sharp turn to the ramp with a well-timed blast of power. Use good judgment in the distance offshore during the parallel approach. If you are too far out when making the 90-degree turn, you will arrive going too fast. If you reduce power then, the wind will turn you away from the ramp, and the diagonal contact may dent the keel on the raised-edge stringer. If you are too near shore, you may turn less than 90 degrees. A good way to judge is to make a trial turn first well offshore to observe the best point to start in and the power needed. Make the final parallel approach enough offshore to coordinate both factors. Or even experiment twice if necessary. It's the mark of an experienced pilot.

Amphibians, of course, use ramps like taxiways. The only problem is wet brakes that don't hold or hold unevenly. It takes power to climb a ramp, and when the level apron is reached, the ship may surge ahead when the brakes are ineffective. Be smart with the throttle. When easing down a ramp to enter the water, the brakes may still be wet. Go slowly so that if one slips, the ship won't yaw to the side. Probably they will chatter, and slow speed saves chatter-strains on the landing gear.

The outboard end of a ramp which is underwater half the time is usually slimy. Locked wheels may slip there, in which case release both and let her roll into the water. A brisk entry will do no harm, except that some tricycle amphibians will bang the sternpost as the bow bobs up. Amphibians with tail wheels should be eased down very cautiously. When the bow is down, the wheels are nearly under the center of gravity and a nose-over is imminent. The bow keel will take such a bump, but the whole ship may yaw sideways, requiring manhandling to realign the plane.

When sliding light seaplanes around a planked ramp on their keels, do not let a keel drop into the gap between planks. Always cross them at a slight angle.

BEACHING

Seaplanes may land at any safe beach in relatively calm water. Any sandy beach devoid of sharp rocks that would seriously scratch the hull bottoms should be safe. You may nose in or drift in from almost any angle and be turned outward by hand by the wading crew. Flying boats that are awash can be turned outward when departing by pulling the wing tip around. Floatplanes are usually tailed to the shore, permitting debarking dry-shod. When possible, it is advisable to inspect the beach in advance to make sure there are no low-tide rocks. If the tide is flooding, you are assured of a takeoff. If it is dropping, you must constantly move the ship to keep her afloat or wait for the tide to come back in. You can wade or swim out and anchor her. Under no conditions, except flat calm and no passing boats, should you attempt a stony beach.

Beaching is also easy for amphibians, and its success depends wholly on the hardness of the sand. If possible, inspect the beach before you use it. If not, approach on an oblique angle so that if it turns out to be soft, the aircraft can be kept moving on an arc back into the water under a lot of power. It is customary to approach with the cabin door side toward shore and to move up only far enough for the

Spencer Amphibian Air Car correctly beached. (Percival Spencer)

passengers to leave dry-shod. The softest sand is always up near the high-tide mark, where it has dried out. The hardest-packed sand is usually near the water's edge, but may be quite soft again at the full low-tide mark, where it often becomes mud instead of sand. Be sure the tail wheel is *unlocked.* It will dig in and stall the whole ship if it is not free to swivel.

A most important item is to have a large tire footprint. To achieve this, deflate the tires as much as possible, only retaining sufficient pressure to prevent their being damaged when landing later on an airport. Do it before using a beach, if possible. If not, do it first to get unstuck.

It is is extremely wise to have a shovel handy!

When taxiing amphibians in unknown shallow water over uncertain bottom, particularly when the water is murky, it is best to extend the wheels for hull protection. However, they must always be lowered in deep water before you enter water that may prove to be shallow. If wheels are extended in shallow water, they may fail parts of the landing gear mechanism should they strike bottom in midposition. Some amphibian gears have fail-safe links intended to shear first before damage, like an outboard's propeller. In that case, the landing gear will be momentarily inoperative until the shear pin is replaced.

8

ADVANCED TECHNIQUES

GLASSY WATER

Glassy water operations are *the most dangerous* in seaplane flying. The surface is a uniform mirror, giving no clue as to your height above. Worse, if it reflects the clouds above, or if there is a slight pattern of decaying waves beneath the mirror, the distortions are dismayingly confusing. The pilot is disarmed by the tranquil surface just when he should be most alert. Judgment of the height above water becomes impossible by observation of the surface alone. Since there is no wind, the contact with the water will be fast. In the absence of wavelets, there will be no lubricating bubbles passing under the hull, and water forces will be maximum.

It is essential that the attitude at touchdown be held steadily and slightly nose up. It is equally essential that the rate of descent also be steady and no more than 150 feet per minute. There are two techniques that will assure attainment of these requirements during the final approach: *visual* and *instrument.* Both require a modicum of steady power.

In the visual approach, the height above water is judged *not* by the indeterminate water surface, but by reference to a pattern of visual objects ahead. It is the easiest and best method except in fog or at night. The water plane can be established in space by sighting any three floating objects spaced moderately apart. When planning the approach for a landing, select a pattern that lies ahead and slightly on the pilot's side. It becomes, then, a visual landing. It is also important to use enough throttle to keep a gradual rate of descent and eliminate the need for flaring. It is *absolutely essential* not to overrun and pass your selected sighting objects while still airborne, lest you find yourself again in a dimensionless void.

A nearby shoreline is an excellent visual guide and the most obvious, because it is usually your destination anyway. A group of boats is just as good or even better. Sometimes floating debris will define the surface. If not, you can make it. Throw rumpled paper, even flight charts, out the window during a low pass (but not too low). You can even use life preservers and retrieve them when you taxi back. The PBY boys used to fire a burst from their fixed gun and land right down the splashes. The renowned Bill Winkapaugh, operating for years out of Rockland, Maine, often made mercy flights into the harbors of offshore islands in cloudy black nights. He would request only that a kerosene lantern be placed in the bottom of a large dory anchored at the start of a clear landing channel. That may sound like a one-point object, but the lighted inside gunnel of the dory established the necessary horizontal plane of reference. It was said he occasionally extinguished the light with the wash from his landing!

The *instrument* method is the most basic. It has been taught the most in the past and will be safe and sure when correctly learned. Unless you are half Indian, like Bill Winkapaugh, it is the only method that will work on a dark night without surface lights. The object is to adjust the power setting and flight speed to fly the airplane about 10 percent above the stalling speed while descending steadily at no more than 150 feet per minute. The airplane then slowly descends in a long straight glide with the nose sufficiently high to make safe contact with the water surface without flare-out. Then the power must be cut promptly before the plane has a chance to fly off again.

This method requires precise piloting. A small variation in air speed results in a considerable change in the rate of descent, which the rate-of-climb indicator is slow to record. A uniform drop in the altimeter is more reliable. Slight changes in power setting have a profound effect and must be correctly adjusted well before the touchdown is anticipated.

The pilot has the advantage of smooth air conditions when the water is glassy, but slight errors in skill result in widely varying vertical velocities. The water may be contacted with quite a thump even when the instrument readings are nearly correct. Be *extremely* careful not to yank back on the wheel or push forward, or do much of anything, except to ease back on the power when the aircraft is surely on the water. Remember, there is an excess of landing speed, enough to fly the airplane back up to a dangerous stalling height if the elevator is raised. If the seaplane leaves the water, it must be flown up to a safe altitude and a new approach made.

The method requires a good deal of room; first, to set up the approach, and second, because the flatness of the approach leaves the actual touchdown point indeterminate. Like any instrument flight procedure, it depends on skill and *must be practiced.* The degree of precision involved in a fast-landing, high-powered seaplane is about comparable to an approach using the Instrument Landing System (ILS), except that the touchdown point need not be as precise as on land.

A precaution on taking off from glassy water should also be observed. Be sure to maintain a steady rate of climb until the altimeter shows a safe altitude. Leveling off too close to the surface may result in inadvertently flying back into it.

The key in this method is to keep everything steady. Rate of change of air speed must be kept slight. We once experimented with two stall-warning horns. One was set for the lowest safe contact speed, and the other for the highest. We believed that would bracket the limits. It did, but it gave no *rate* information. We still had to maintain steady attentive flying. If we had pierced either limit with a fast divergence just before contact, there would have been a disastrous landing.

A few additional remarks have a bearing on this operation. If the pilot's seat in a flying boat is near the leading edge of the wing, and you have a wide angle of vision, you can detect the final proximity to the water by seeing the reflection of the wing out of the corner of the eye. But don't *look* at it. Use this cue only as a signal as to your progress down the glide slope. It merely tells you that touchdown is seconds ahead. If you are thoroughly familiar with the feel of the airplane, there is another cue. When the ground cushion builds up between the wing and the water there is a small but perceptible change in the attitude as the downwash airflow changes. It is a useful signal but cannot be used to "feel" for the water. A ground (water) cushion becomes effective only when the wing is no higher than twice the wing chord. Thus, it helps little on high-wing floatplanes.

Glassy water may also produce strange illusions. If there are scattered clouds overhead, their reflections will "travel along under you"—and lead you to think you are in a hovering helicopter! If sky conditions permit you to see down to the bottom in clear water, there is an almost irresistible desire to look at it right at the crucial time. Don't!

If the bottom is ten feet deep, you are almost sure to impact the water ten feet too soon and ricochet. In mountain areas, lakes are very often placidly calm. If you use the shoreline as a visual reference, be sure to look only at the shoreline and disregard the inverted skyline reflections. Since the bearings on the skyline are changing slowly, there is a tendency to turn slightly toward the shore.

When making either visual or instrument approaches, be sure your passengers don't romp around behind you and disturb the steady trim angle you have established.

You may well ask, "When should I use which?" In forty-two years of flying, with at least half the hours flown in seaplanes, I have often practiced and checked others on instrument letdowns to glassy water in such places as the middle of Long Island Sound, Lake Ontario, and off the Cuban shore. However, *I have never HAD to make even one!* The reason should be obvious. No one ever has a flight objective to such places. There is nothing out there to go to. (Perhaps there is an exception; several times after a practice session, we have all gone overboard and taken skinny-dips.) We use seaplanes to fly to where we want to go. Always, in daytime, that is a visual objective we can use to set up a safe letdown. Does that answer the question?

Whether used or not, the practice of making instrument letdowns is valuable experience in steadying your power and trim controls during visual letdowns. Practice them.

I should confess I once made a glassy-water landing at night—and dead-stick at that. (A forced landing without power is termed "dead-stick" because the prop, or "stick," is stopped.) It was in a Viking Flying Boat in New Haven Harbor with Ray Quick, who was the examining test pilot for the then Aeronautics Branch of the Department of Commerce, now the FAA. We were seeking the Approved Type Certificate authorizing production.

In three days of flying Ray had confirmed all of my

previous test flights. Though he had been concerned about the fuel feed, we felt the certificate was just about in our hands. The fuel was drawn from a single tank in the hull by a pump on the Wright J–6–7 engine in a nacelle between the wings more than three feet above. During a late lunch on the day before Thanksgiving, Ray dashed our hopes by requesting we make a test rig duplicating the system and permitting the test tank to be tilted violently. He wanted to determine if the pump would still empty the tank when the level was so low air might enter the feed line. He could not return for two weeks to witness the test.

To me, it seemed simpler to try it out on the airplane in flight. We'd take off with very low fuel, skid, climb, and dive the ship until the engine quit, then measure the remaining fuel after a boat towed us back to the ramp. Ray reluctantly agreed, though he was anxious to leave for the long weekend. By the time we syphoned the tank down to what we thought was two remaining gallons, the sun had set behind low clouds.

The water was scuffed from a light breeze as we took off for the expected short flight. The coming dead-stick landing held no dread for me. At 1000 feet we made large figure-eights over New Haven's outer harbor while every few minutes Ray pushed violently on rudder and wheel alternately, attempting to slosh the fuel in the tank.

The faithful Wright droned on. The cloud layer spread above us. Street lights winked on around the harbor. Ray flew more wildly. The wind dropped, and in the last gloom I noted glassy water below. Still the engine ran. Then it was full dark night. When would the darned fuel run out? How would I find the water surface? Should we land while we still had power, or should we hang on to win the coveted certificate now? It was obvious there were many more than two gallons in the tank when we took off. We noted a brightly lighted tanker departing the harbor at full speed.

Though we could not see her wake in the darkness, I knew it was spreading into the area I expected to land, and I had no desire to land into those waves. We moved farther out beyond her, but now we were nearly two miles from the shore lights.

At last, just as we were turning away from the lighted city, the engine quit cold without a sputter. In the darkness, Ray tapped my knee. It was time for me to fly! I could imagine his half smile, but guessed his brow was as wrinkled as my own with apprehension.

Wire-braced biplanes had very low L/Ds—the ratio of *lift* to *drag*. The reciprocal—the D/L—is the *angle of glide*, which was then always quite steep. In a gliding turn we faced the distant city and settled into the blackness below, the tanker's lights now too far off our port wing to help. It wasn't quite a blind landing; the distant lights gave us a horizon but no help in determining when to flare for the touchdown.

But we did—somehow—and though with a good thump, we stayed on the water. The landing was "adequate." Without a word, Ray lit a cigarette and sat on the combing while we waited for our stand-by boat. She had watched our running lights and soon towed us in. While Ray and the crew determined there was not a drop of gas remaining in the tank, I was busy arguing with two waiting burly New Haven policemen that the many reports of crazy drunken flying over the harbor were utterly unfounded.

The ATC was ours. But I wouldn't attempt such a landing in a modern seaplane.

There is at least one place in the world where night water landings are easier than day: New York's East River under the bridges. The water surface there is always a confused mass of intersecting wave patterns from passing boats, mixed with waves from boats long passed and now reflected back out from the piers. Pilots, sitting low in small flying boats, have occasionally observed "chunks" of water as big as basketballs thrown a foot or more in the air by three or more waves impacting at a common point. Strangely, although the same surface prevails at night, it looks better. It is uniformly floodlighted by a million lighted windows in the skyscrapers. (Cleaning women kept them lighted throughout the night, before the fuel shortage.) No airport runway in the world is so well illuminated.

This is a timely point to interject another item. A very few seaplanes have sunk in the East River, but only as the result of collisions or stupid piloting that would have sunk them anywhere else. The water is loaded with giant brickbats, including wharf piles and railroad ties, that have on rare occasions slightly damaged seaplanes operating there. But according to a survey made in 1960, there was no recorded case of sinking as a result of all this debris. Remember, seaplanes can make sharp enough turns on the water to dodge flotsam.

ROUGH WATER

Marine airplanes are designed to fly from one relatively sheltered body of water to another. Landings in open rough-water areas are just as much emergencies as landing large landplanes in unprepared pastures. A pilot's ability to operate in relatively rough water grows with experience. It is based mostly on an understanding of wave propagation and wave patterns, and accurate recognition of them from above. This requires judgment, and the ability to control the airplane skillfully is secondary. An exception is landing on large open ocean swells; skill is then of prime importance. Small marine airplanes and unprofessional pilots have no business, or probable need, to land out there.

Because of their larger hull and greater compactness, flying boats have better seagoing capability than floatplanes. The strength of the hull bottom is usually the limiting factor. Accelerometers on the bottom plates often record "G" loads in excess of six, though these may be reduced to four at the pilot's seat and even lower at the wing level due to the absorbing flexibility of the structure between.

WIND AND HOW IT IS RATED

Wind is the force that generates waves. It sculptures the sea into complex corrugations that seem to baffle analysis. However, since the 1930s, great progress has been accomplished in this science. General acceptance of the Beaufort Scale of Wind Forces initiated this work, followed by coordination of velocity and effects (see figure 7). The table is worthy of careful study and repeated consultation. It has been reproduced so often that the source is unknown to this author.

WAVES AND HOW THEY GROW

The equally important table on wind waves at sea (figure 8) goes further in coordinating wave characteristics with the wind. It was developed by the General Electric Advanced Technology Laboratory and authenticated by the Woods Hole Oceanographic Institute.

WAVE GENERATION

The surface tension of calm water resists distortion until increasing breezes attain about two knots; then ripples are formed in patches. But if the wind returns to zero, the water viscosity promptly damps the ripples and the surface returns

Beaufort Scale and Map Symbol	*Terms Used by U.S. Weather Bureau*	*Velocity mph*	*Estimating Velocities on Land*
0	Calm	Less than 1	Smoke rises vertically.
1	Light air	1 —3	Smoke drifts; wind vanes unmoved.
2	Light Breeze	4 —7	Wind felt on face; leaves rustle; ordinary vane moves by wind.
3	Gentle Breeze	8 —12	Leaves and small twigs in constant motion; wind extends light flag.
4	Moderate Breeze	13—18	Dust and loose paper raised; small branches are moved.
5	Fresh Breeze	19—24	Small trees in leaf begin to sway; crested wavelets form in inland water.
6	Strong Breeze	25—31	Large branches in motion; whistling heard in telegraph wires; umbrellas used with difficulty.
7	Moderate Gale	32—38	Whole trees in motion; inconvenience felt in walking against the wind.
8	Fresh Gale	39—46	Twigs broken off trees; Progress generally impeded.
9	Strong Gale	47—54	Slight structural damage occurs.
10	Whole Gale	55—63	Trees uprooted; considerable structural damage occurs.
11		64—75	
12	Hurricane	Above 75	

1. Long and straight wind streaks indicate that wind is steady in force and direction.
2. Curved streaks indicate possible change of wind direction.
3. Distinct line on surface, as if caused by rip tide, indicates possible reversal of wind direction.
4. Although surface appearance may appear the same, wind force in open sea is usually stronger than in adjace sheltered waters.

Estimating Velocities on Sea	
Sea like a mirror.	Check your glassy water technique before water flying under these conditions.
Ripples with the appearance of scales are formed but without foam crests.	
Small wavelets, still short but more pronounced; crests have a glassy appearance and do not break.	
Large wavelets; crests begin to break. Foam of glassy appearance. (Perhaps scattered whitecaps.)	Ideal water flying characteristics in protected water.
Small waves, becoming longer; fairly frequent whitecaps.	
Moderate waves, taking a more pronounced long form; many whitecaps are formed. (Chance of some spray.)	This is considered rough water for seaplanes and small amphibians, especially in open water.
Large waves begin to form; white foam crests are more extensive everywhere. (Probably some spray.)	
Sea heaps up and white foam from breaking waves begins to be blown in streaks along the direction of the wind.	This type of water condition is for emergency only in small aircraft in inland waters and for the expert pilot of the large military and naval flying boats in the open sea.
Moderately high waves of greater length; edges of crests break into spindrift. The foam is blown in well-marked streaks along the direction of the wind.	It's now time to be careful of land landings and takeoffs.
High waves; dense streaks of foam along the direction of the wind. Sea begins to roll. Spray may affect visibility.	
Very high waves with long, overhanging crests. The resulting foam, in great patches, is blown in dense white streaks along the direction of the wind. On the whole, the surface of the sea takes a white appearance. The rolling of the sea becomes heavy and shock-like. Visibility is affected.	

Figure 7—Wind Chart

Figure 8—Wind Waves at Sea

1 WIND VELOCITY KNOTS	4, 5, 6, 7, 8, 9, 10, 20, 30, 40, 50, 60, 70
2 BEAUFORT WIND AND DESCRIPTION	1 LIGHT AIR; 2 LIGHT BREEZE; 3 GENTLE BREEZE; 4 MODERATE BREEZE; 5 FRESH BREEZE; 6 STRONG BREEZE; 7 MODERATE GALE; 8 FRESH GALE; 9 STRONG GALE; 10 WHOLE GALE; 11 STORM
3 REQUIRED FETCH IN MILES	FETCH IS THE NUMBER OF MILES A GIVEN WIND HAS BEEN BLOWING OVER OPEN WATER — 50, 100, 200, 300, 400, 500, 600, 700
4 REQUIRED WIND DURATION IN HOURS	DURATION IS THE TIME A GIVEN WIND HAS BEEN BLOWING OVER OPEN WATER — 5, 20, 25, 30, 35

IF THE FETCH AND DURATION ARE AS GREAT AS INDICATED ABOVE, THE FOLLOWING WAVE CONDITIONS WILL EXIST. WAVE HEIGHTS MAY BE UP TO 10% GREATER IF FETCH AND DURATION ARE GREATER.

5 WAVE HEIGHT CREST TO TROUGH IN FEET	2, 4 (WHITE CAPS FORM), 6, 8, 10, 15, 20, 25, 30, 40, 50, 60
6 SEA STATE AND DESCRIPTION	1 SMOOTH; 2 SLIGHT; 3 MODER-ATE; 4 ROUGH; 5 VERY ROUGH; 6 HIGH; 7 VERY HIGH; 8 PRECIPITOUS
7 WAVE PERIOD SEC.	1, 2, 3, 4, 6, 8, 10, 12, 14, 16, 18, 20
8 WAVE LENGTH FEET	20, 40, 60, 80, 100, 150, 200, 300, 400, 500, 600, 800, 1000, 1400, 1800
9 WAVE VELOCITY KNOTS	5, 10, 15, 20, 25, 30, 35, 40, 45, 50, 55, 60
10 PARTICLE VELOCITY FEET/SEC.	1, 2, 3, 4, 5, 6, 8, 10, 12, 14
11 WIND VELOCITY KNOTS	4, 5, 6, 7, 8, 9, 10, 20, 30, 40, 50, 60, 70

This table applies only to waves generated by the local wind and does not apply to swell originating elsewhere.

WARNING: Presence of swell makes accurate wave observations exceedingly difficult.

NOTE: (a) *The height of waves is arbitrarily chosen as the height of the highest 1/3 of the waves. Occasional waves caused by interference between waves or between waves and swell may be considerably larger.*

(b) *Only lines 7, 8, and 9 are applicable to swell as well as waves.*

(c) *The above values are only approximate due both to lack of precise data and to the difficulty in expressing it in a single easy way.*

(d) *Below the surface the wave motion decreases by 1/2 for every 1/9 of a wave length of depth increase.*

(e) *Observations and comments leading to increased accuracy and usefulness are desired.*

Publication suggested by J. Pritzlaff, General Electric Advanced Technology Lab., Schenectady, N.Y.

to a flat calm. If the wind strengthens to four knots, the ripples become small waves that persist for some time after the breeze has stopped blowing.

When the wind increases more, the sea surface is carpeted with a complicated pattern of waves, the heights, periods, and speeds of which appear to be varying continually between wide limits. This is the *generating area.* An established wave affects the water mass ahead and behind, so that a train of waves is formed. They become larger and travel faster. It is inevitable that some trains will not synchronize as early as others and their advance will be slower. Thus, the earlier trains advance in a crescent-shaped front. Where two well-established trains border each other, the later trains will have to merge in short-lived confusion before they enlarge and keep pace with the others. The generating area is often called a *choppy sea.* In Newfoundland, it is called a "lop"—and it looks it!

The generating area remains confused as long as the wind is increasing and the waves become larger. When the wind settles to a constant velocity, waves also settle into a more uniform pattern and size. Their characteristics become better defined and conform to a science. In Newfoundland the sea is now called an "ippety lop."

Now the waves consist of a series of equidistant parallel crests, of the same height. For analysis purposes, it is assumed they move without change of shape, at constant speed in a direction perpendicular to the line of the crests. A section through these waves is known to engineers as a trochoidal curve, the curve traced out by a point on the spoke of a wheel which rolls along a horizontal line. This curve differs from a sine curve in that the crest is steeper and the trough flatter (see figure 9).

Observation of a body floating on the surface of water over which a train of simple waves is moving shows that the

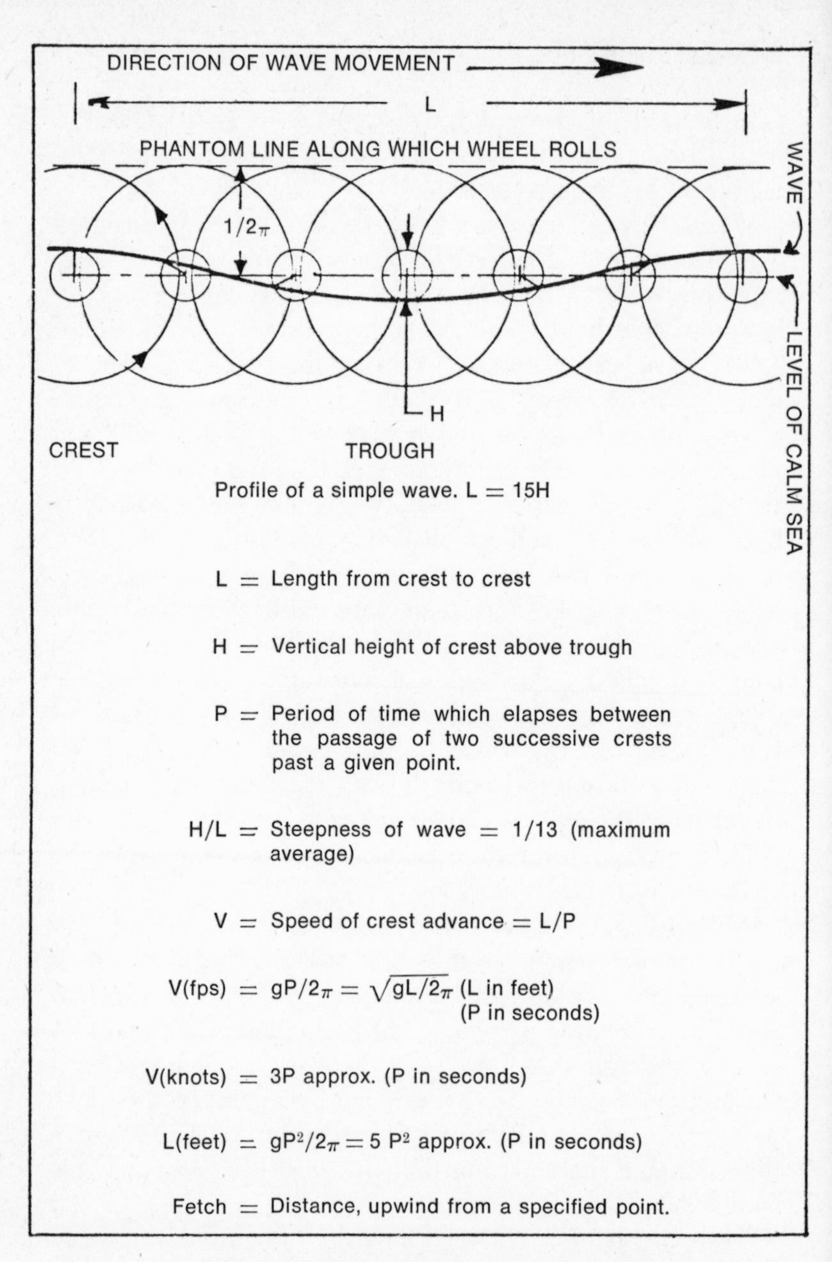

Figure 9—Wave Shape and Formulae

water itself does not move along with the waves. The floating body will describe a circle in a vertical plane, moving upward as the crest approaches, forward as the crest passes, downward as the crest recedes, and backward as the trough passes. It ends up after the passage of each wave almost where it started. The actual movement of an element of water at the surface is a vertical circle whose diameter is equal to the height of the wave. This statement must be slightly modified because the tangential friction of the wind on the whole water surface produces a slow flow of water downwind known as the *drift*. It explains why a nearly submerged log will slowly drift with the waves. In deep water, wave motion causes some disturbance below the surface which penetrates little deeper than half the wave length.

As the wind speed and energy increase, the "rolling wheel" becomes larger before the length begins to increase. The waves rapidly become steeper. Steepness is defined as the ratio of height to length, or H/L. Waves generated by a steady wind up to about 12 knots have an average steepness of about 7 percent. When the wind and the drive increase further, the steepness will reach a maximum of 10 to 12 percent. The crest will no longer maintain a smooth curve. It will become a cusp and "break." That is, foam will form at the crest and become a *whitecap*. When the wind starts to decrease, the waves may remain just as high, but since they have now lengthened, the whitecaps disappear. A little *froth* will appear on the surface before the whitecap stage. It tends to persist in the form of small bubbles that coalesce in lines that blow straight downwind, forming wind streaks. When seen from above, these streaks are an accurate indication of wind direction.

Fetch is the distance the wind has blown to form a wave pattern. Waves generated by winds of 10 knots run about a foot high and do not further increase, regardless of the fetch. When winds exceed 12 to 15 knots, waves continue to grow in proportion to the lengthening fetch.

It takes a lot of wind energy to create a heavy sea, but when the wind stops, the energy persists and is damped out only by the very slight internal friction in the water. Wave patterns continue long distances from their source and diminish at a barely perceptible rate. They are then called *swells*, gradually lengthening, gradually becoming less high, but always increasing in speed. Wave patterns generated by a cyclone in the western Pacific have been traced by the recorded swell data all the way to the North American coast.

Waves or swells are practically always present in the open sea. It is common to find areas in the deep sea where the wind direction has changed and may be blowing parallel to the crests, or even against them. This will cause an entirely separate wave pattern, or sea, superimposed on the swell. Occasionally a crosswind will produce three distinctive patterns, easily detected from an airplane though hard to see from a boat on the surface.

The size of waves is affected by islands, shoals, and tidal currents. An island with steep shores allows the seas to pass with little distortion, creating a relatively calm surface on the lee shore. But if the extremities of the island have outlying shoals, causing the near waves to break and slow down, the trains farther out will be refracted around and behind, and remain high. In the center of the lee side, the waves coming around from both ends will meet, producing a choppy sea.

Frequently, shoals exist offshore where the water shallows and then becomes deep again. The waves steepen on the shoal, and if the water is shallow enough, they will break. This breaking will cause a considerable loss of height on the lee side of the shoal. However, if the waves do not break on the shoal, there will be little reduction in wave size after they have crossed it.

When waves generated in nonflowing water travel into moving water, they undergo important changes. If the current is moving in the same direction as the waves, they increase in speed and length and lose height. But if the water is moving opposite to the waves, they will decrease in speed and length, but will gain height and steepen. This explains the well-known tidal rips formed where strong tidal streams run against the waves. A current of six mph will break most waves running against it, unless they are very long and low. If breaking occurs in the stream, there will be a considerable diminution in height of the waves to leeward of the breaking area.

ROUGH-WATER TECHNIQUE

The beating a marine aircraft takes in rough water is best measured by the steepness of the waves and the speed of contact. As we have seen, a freshly created sea blown by a strong wind will have steep, short waves. A subsiding seaway left over from previous winds will have long waves with less steep slopes, but they will be moving faster. The speed of contact is the combination of the speed of the advancing sea and the airplane's landing speed, which is, of course, basically dependent on the speed of the wind. In a really rough seaway, with all these variables present, only a lot of experience will enable a pilot to decide whether an upwind, up-sea landing, or a crosswind, along-the-crests landing, or even a downwind landing is best. Further complications occur when the wind and the seas are moving in different directions and when the chop and the swells run in odd directions.

Wave lengths are measured from the crest of one wave to the crest of the following wave. The best way to judge wave lengths is to compare them to the airplane's hull length. If a wave length is half the hull length or less, the hull will be supported on the water in two or more places at once and, consequently, the amount of pitching experienced will be relatively little. However, in wave lengths approximately two times the hull length, the hull is never carried by more than one wave crest at any time. Obviously, the hull will not quite fit between two wave crests, and once it is over a crest, it will pitch down into the trough. In waves of more than three to four hull lengths, the airplane can be flown parallel to the crests and troughs fairly easily, depending on the amount of wind. Consequently, the wave contours become easier to cope with.

Even a seaway that has left the generating area and has become quite regular still has some interference areas where well-defined wave trains advancing at slightly different speeds intersect. Where crests coincide, they reinforce each other and groups of relatively high waves appear. Where the crests of one train coincide with the troughs of the other, a partial cancellation occurs and the resulting waves are low. This effect substantiates the oft-repeated observation that every third wave is larger and every ninth wave is a whopper—although the count is not *that* accurate. Figure 10 shows a typical pattern.

These isolated smooth areas can be used to very good advantage in moderate-sized windswept lakes and bays. In landing, they can be detected by bringing the airplane down to about 10 feet and then dragging under power until a somewhat smoother spot shows up ahead. Then cut the throttle completely and land right up to it, or even a bit short of it, at minimum speed. In takeoffs, wait with idling throttle and study the waves ahead. After a few minutes, a

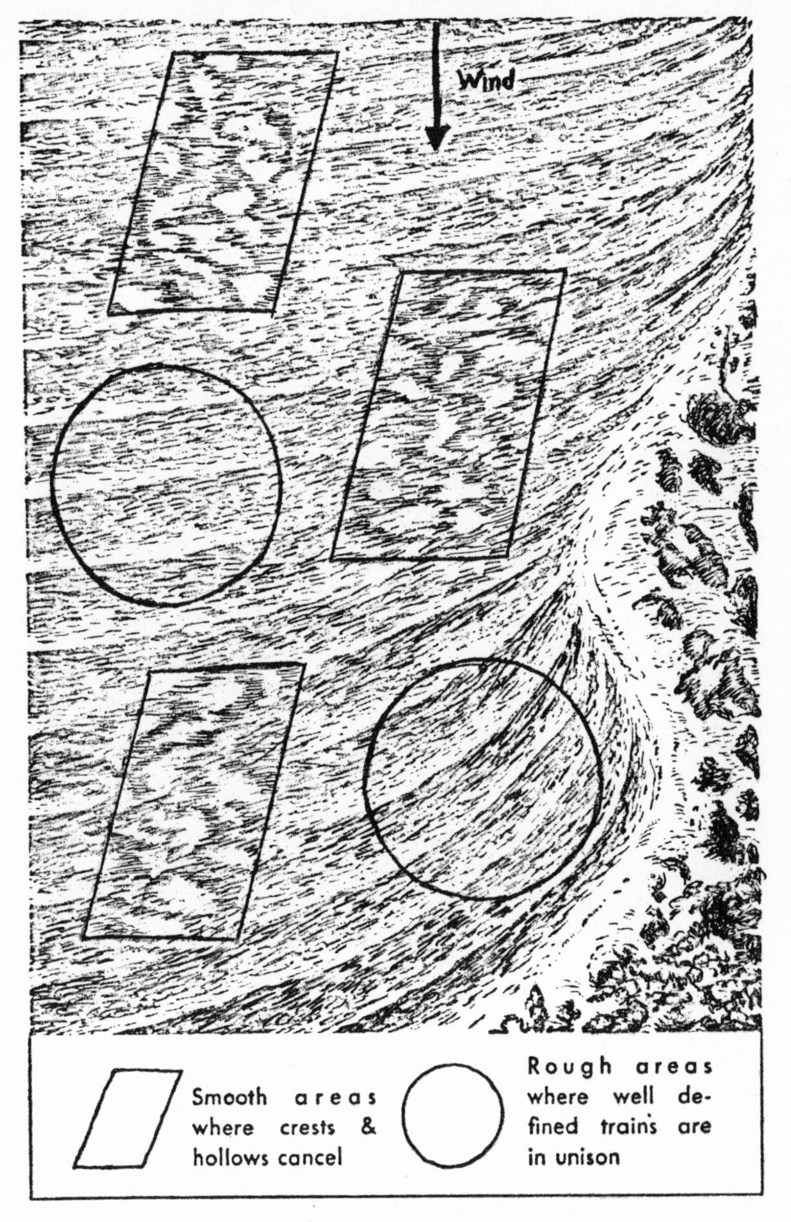

Figure 10—Wave Trains

reduction in wave height frequently may be detected and the takeoff can be started so that the critical spray-throwing speed will occur in this smoother area.

There is little that can be said to help a pilot develop skill in controlling an airplane sliding over a rough sea. It is just a case of learning the feel and developing alert responses through experience. Landings are easier than takeoffs in lightly loaded, low-powered airplanes, because the takeoff runs are longer. In high-powered planes with heavier wing loadings, the worst beating usually occurs during the middle third of the landing run, because speed is still excessive, but too low for the elevator controls to help ease the bouncing. In such airplanes, the takeoffs are fairly quick and the strong slipstream on the tail surfaces provides effective control response. The basic problem is to keep the airplane at the correct attitude despite the pounding.

If the above considerations appear to limit seaplane utility, remember there are infinitely more sheltered harbors and lakes than airports, and that most places can be reached without having to consider rough water.

THE DEEP SEA

Operations in the open sea should be confined to only the largest amphibians or seaplanes with highly skilled water pilots and should be attempted only for emergency or rescue purposes. The gross weight should be kept to a minimum, in order to reduce the impact forces and speeds.

The following procedures and techniques have been adapted from US Coast Guard and Air Force recommendations and are presented here to illustrate the difference between deep-sea and inshore sheltered-water operations.

The best direction for a landing or takeoff in a well-defined swell with winds of less than 12 mph is parallel to the swell.

In the presence of several definite wave systems, the sea should be studied very carefully by the pilot and an attempt made to land on a heading which will not run directly into the face of either wave system and which will bring the wind on the bow rather than on the quarter, if it cannot be brought ahead. Such conditions are very difficult and dangerous, and the pilot should be alert for the unexpected. Whenever possible, landings made parallel to the swells should be directed so that the swell front is moving toward the port side of the airplane to observe the existing sea conditions more readily. A landing can be made with safety parallel to the swell either on the crest or in the trough.

The second-best choice for landing or takeoff is downswell. The object here is to obtain minimum relative speed between aircraft and swells. If the swell has greater speed than the wind and is coming from the same direction, the algebraic total effect of swell and wind speeds will be most favorable to an aircraft heading downswell and downwind. For example, with swell 30 mph and wind 10 mph in the same direction, an airplane landing at 60 mph airspeed will have a relative speed over the swells of 40 mph if landed downswell, or 80 mph if landed upswell.

Landings or takeoffs into swell and wind are poor third choices unless the wind is faster than the swell. Heading should be made to bring wind as much ahead as possible without driving directly into the swells. However, at wind velocities above 20 mph, surface conditions in the open sea generally are such as to make any landing impractical.

In a confused sea, landings and takeoffs should be made on a heading that will not point the airplane directly into any swell system, while heading into the wind as closely as possible.

The desired landing for rough-water operation is to have the airplane touch down in a nose-high attitude. In order to accomplish this technique, a normal approach is made with full flaps down and props in low pitch. Four or five feet above the water, establish a slow-flying attitude, nose high. Fly just above the water until the desired landing spot appears; close the throttles, raise the nose of the airplane, and stall onto the water. In a well-stalled landing, the runout will begin easily, but damage may result in bouncing after landing. Holding the nose high or applying power results in attainment of increased height and a harder subsequent impact. Therefore, although the airplane makes first contact with the nose held high, the nose should be lowered to a horizontal pitch angle during the runout, since:

1. The airplane will slow down sooner due to greater immersed hull area and increased surface friction.
2. The airplane will leave the swell slope at a lower angle of attack and will gain less height. To hold the airplane on in this manner, the pilot must have quick reactions and must lead with the elevators in order to have the airplane's nose in the right attitude at each moment during riding up and down successive swell slopes.
3. If reversible propellers are available, they should be used to shorten the runout.

Judging open-sea conditions by eye is very difficult, because a locally formed sea may conceal a long, fast swell beneath it. Observers usually underestimate the length of most swells and the height of low swells and overestimate the height of big swells.

To obtain the velocity and length of swell, fly at an altitude of 2000 feet and drop a float light or smoke bomb and then circle it, timing and counting its passage over successive crests. The time in seconds divided by the number of crests gives the period in seconds of each wave. Multiply period in seconds by three to obtain velocity of swell in knots. Multiply square of period in seconds by five to obtain length of swell in feet.

Fly at low altitude (about 200 feet) and note if direction of swell agrees with that obtained at 2000 feet. If not, there may be two swell systems from different directions, or a second swell system may be superimposed on the first, but coming from the same direction. This condition may be indicated by the presence of periodic groups of swells larger than average.

Fly low on several likely headings and note on which one the sea appears most favorable for landing. The heading that looks smoothest should be the best, provided that it is not opposite to the direction of the swells previously observed, and due consideration is given to the velocity of the ground swell. Try to set the aircraft down on the near edge of this smooth area at minimum speed. Beware of missing a swell crest while stalled and falling several feet more than intended into the trough.

In takeoff, the same general principles that apply to landing are involved. The roughest period usually occurs before attaining enough speed for firm elevator and aileron control. The pilot may have to start his run downwind and then turn to the takeoff heading. Starting the takeoff on the desired heading will probably be easiest.

On a heading parallel to crests, start on top of a crest; whenever possible, have the swell advancing from the port beam to enable the pilot to see the existing sea conditions more readily. As the swell advances, the pilot may either ease the nose of the airplane slightly downswell in an effort to keep the airplane on top of the crest throughout the run, or he may steer a course parallel to the crest. The airplane should be lifted off immediately upon reaching flying speed. Even though it may touch successive wave crests, the impact will be slight, when the nose-up pitch angle is moderate.

If takeoff heading is downswell, the pilot should accelerate the airplane gradually, riding the nose up and down successive swells, keeping the speed low enough to avoid leaving the water prematurely. Try to keep the airplane in the attitude at which it accelerates best with regard to the water surface under it. The pilot should remember that the taxi speed attained before full throttle is applied is so much to the good. When the airplane is just below takeoff speed and is at the top of a big swell with smaller swells ahead, the pilot should open throttle smartly in an effort to obtain takeoff and to stay in the air when the airplane reaches the top of the next swell ahead. Under complex sea conditions, choose a heading that will:

1. Avoid running directly into the face of any swell system.
2. Bring wind ahead as much as possible.
3. Involve minimum of taxied turns out of wind.

When a pilot feels it necessary to take off into a long, fast swell, which is not a recommended procedure, he will find that the swells seem very close together and very high, because the airplane is crossing a maximum number of crests in a minimum of time. Attempts by the pilot to jockey the nose of the airplane over the swells are especially difficult under such conditions, because he is crossing the swells so rapidly at low airspeed and with little control.

In rough water, damage to wing-tip floats is possible, and during taxiing, power must be applied sparingly to prevent shearing off a float. Also, in strong winds it is difficult to turn the airplane downwind, and attempts to do so may result in damage to a float. The airplane will almost certainly capsize if a float is lost or becomes filled with water, unless sufficient men can be put on the opposite wing quickly enough to keep the damaged wing off the water.

In case of damage received during a takeoff or attempted takeoff, the decision to continue the takeoff or to cut the throttles must be made instantaneously. It will depend upon all the factors involved in the situation, of which the principal ones are: If takeoff is to continue, will the airplane be able to maintain flight? If takeoff is discontinued, will the airplane remain afloat?

ACCIDENTS

A study of water-landing accidents strongly indicates that abuse of power is a fundamental cause. Rarely does a one-point crash occur. Nearly always, the first contacts are quite satisfactory, after which a series of bounces or swerves occurs, getting higher and harder until the crackup.

Finding the surface of the water is not the basic trouble. Too much power at the wrong time generally causes trouble. On both rough water and glassy water, the pilot is trying hard to land the airplane when the engines are furnishing nearly enough power to fly it. Experienced pilots may sometimes be able to soften a bounce by applying a short, quick blast of power, but this procedure can very easily be overdone. Since a power-on approach to glassy water starts with a moderately high power setting, it is not surprising that power difficulties may follow the touchdown.

It takes a lot of energy to crack up an airplane, particularly on a somewhat yielding water surface. That energy is measured by the weight and the square of the velocity. Speed must be kept minimum. Pilots, particularly beginners in water flying, should not feed any more energy into the picture by using throttle. If a landing is messed up to a point where only a blast of power will prevent disaster, then full power should be applied and the airplane flown around for another approach.

One often hears of "hooking" or "stubbing" a wing-tip float, with the common misconception that the nose of the float gets down and dives under. A little thought will show that this cannot be the case. The angle at which all wing-tip floats are attached always considerably exceeds the keel angle itself; hence, if a float ever actually "hooked," the hull would also be diving under. In very rough seas at slow taxiing speeds, large waves often completely submerge a float. But tip floats are so streamlined that even when buried, they will not exert a very large drag force. If they hit waves at high speed, very large vertical loads will be created on them, but the rearward loads will be less.

When an airplane water loops, say to port, the starboard float is slammed down by the centrifugal force. The very high vertical loads soon fail the struts, and the wing and crippled float plunge into the water. This creates a large drag force, swerving the airplane sharply back to starboard. The airplane comes to rest pointing to starboard of its original course with that wing damaged and in the water, and the usual analysis is that it "hooked" the starboard wing-tip float. *That* was a water loop to *port*!

9

HELPFUL INFORMATION

EQUIPMENT

Every airplane should carry a few basic tools and a flashlight, and that's about all a landplane needs. Seaplanes need most of the standard marine equipment found in small boats. *Life preservers* for each person are required by law and also by common sense. Use the buckle-on type, not the little cushions used in outboards, but if you need cabin cushions for other reasons, they might as well contain kapok and handle-straps. Stow them under the seats far enough aft so they won't foul floor controls, or in an open luggage compartment, quickly accessible from the cabin. When you feel you may be heading into danger, request your passengers to wear them, just as you would in a small boat.

ANCHORS

Carry at least one lightweight semifolding anchor. Danforth anchors are the most popular. A single anchor should weigh about: 10 pounds for a 2000-pound seaplane; 20 pounds for 5000 pounds; 30 pounds for 10,000 pounds.

Larger seaplanes rarely carry anchors large enough to hold them in a steady blow, because they usually operate from bases or moorings, though they still carry "lunch-hook"-size anchors adequate to hold them in good weather while transferring passengers from small boats. Nylon anchor lines should be strength rated for about two-thirds the weight of the seaplane and at least 150 feet long. Polypropaline lines weigh less, even float on the water, but they are a bit kinky to coil. Anchors, and the carefully coiled line, should be stowed in float or bow compartments. If there is no other equipment in the compartment, the lines may be "flaked" below the anchor to pay out quickly. Always secure the bitter end before heaving. If you carry two anchors, a second line is of course required.

Once we almost crunched a Viking because my friend and flying partner, the renowned George Wiess, failed to heed this admonition. We were delivering the first of the Coast Guard Viking fleet to the base at Cape May, New Jersey. It was a bitter day with a strong west wind, and we were shivering in the open cockpit. At last the Coast Guard Station came in sight far ahead—and just then the engine quit cold! We landed easily in a lagoon behind the Jersey beaches, and scurried to get out the anchor.

The high wind drifted us backwards so fast we were making bow waves off the stern. Our downwind drift was heading our delicate tail surfaces straight for what must have been the only pile of rocks on that coast. It was clear we were in very shallow water with a hard mud bottom, because the anchor flukes were sliding over it without grabbing. Since George had thrown the anchor, I jumped on the lower wing to wind up the old inertia starter, hoping to get at least a small burst of power before it was too late.

While facing the tail and grinding desperately on the crank, the ship suddenly checked her mad rush. I looked forward to see George slowly being pulled over the windshield until his lanky frame was stretched far out over the bow with his extended hands squeezed around the last six inches of the anchor line. For a moment it looked as if the anchor and the ship were lost. I cared little for George's own welfare at the moment! Fortunately his long legs remained behind in the cockpit. At the last moment, his heels raised with a whack under the back of the cockpit combing—and held. We were safely anchored, but it took me a piece to haul George back, first by his belt, then his collar, and finally his clenched hands.

We cleated the line, and in a few minutes a couple of spray-drenched boys came alongside in an outboard as they always do. We asked them to phone the Coast Guard and tell them where we were. In about an hour a Coast Guard boat entered the lagoon and sent a dinghy in over the mud bank with a long line, and we delivered the new seaplane to the Coast Guard in deep humiliation at the end of their own tow-rope.

The moral is to make the bitter end fast unless you have, like George, a six-foot six-inch frame.

HANDLING LINES

Two light 3/8-inch lines about 40 feet long should be carried for docking and general purposes. They are sometimes called "throw lines." Many floatplanes keep a short length of line permanently cleated to each bow, extending back just short of the point where they could intersect the propeller disc and offering little drag in flight, lying smooth on the float deck. Floatplanes should carry a bridle for anchoring and towing purposes. Each leg should be long enough to make a 30-degree angle from the extended center line of the float to the eye of the bridle, which is usually a chromed or bronze ring. All lines should terminate in a spliced eye on one end, just large enough to fit over the cleats, with a snaphook on the other end. The snaphook will have about the right weight for heaving, but heave the spliced end if the receiver is standing in front of a windshield! Bronze snaphooks and shackles are as strong as the nylon line they are sized for. Avoid galvanized hardware, which is weaker and may bend open. Bronze is nearly inert, but over a long period it may corrode aluminum when it is in constant contact. Leave the hook within the coil or glue a small pad on the aluminum where the hook rests.

OTHER EQUIPMENT

A short *boathook* is optional, but a very great help at times. Many floatplanes carry a boathook on the end of a *paddle* and slip it under a clamp and pin on the float deck. Caution the man in the bow hatch of a flying boat not to let the end of the boathook pass over his shoulder and possibly into a spinning prop behind.

If operations include fueling while in the water or in remote places, always carry a *funnel* with a straining *chamois skin* spread across the hopper.

Every boat, even fiberglass, is subject to slow leaks. Provisions for pumping are essential. Most seaplanes carry small *boat pumps.* Big flying boats need hose extensions long enough to spill overboard from any compartment. Many Edo floats have built-in tubes from the bottom of each compartment leading to the deck, where they terminate in a female rubber cone. The supply pump has a mating male wedge permitting quick check or water removal without removing the compartment handhold cover. Remember to replace the plugs closing these tubes at the deck.

Most amphibians have *screw plugs* through the bottom at the low point of each compartment. It is common practice to check or drain these when next on land after a period afloat. A beautiful Widgeon disappeared once after picking up a mooring on the Coast. She was found on the bottom. You guessed it: the plugs had been left out by a careless mechanic, and the party had left the mooring area before she settled enough for anyone to notice. The life of an insurance adjuster is not easy.

If you fly even to the fringes of the bush, it is wise to carry an *inflatable dinghy* and an *air pump* if there are no CO_2 inflating cartridges. Beside being important safety items—and several dinghies have been used in ditching landplanes between the Bahamas and the mainland—they are essential wherever you must be independent of shore help.

There are many other ingenious devices that various owners consider essential. You'll have fun making your own. In Mallards I always carried a short lightweight fabric ladder that slipped over the cleat and hung over the bow. It was handy in boarding over the rounded bow from beaches or low docks.

TRICKS

On a full-load takeoff from glassy water at a high-altitude lake on a hot day, you may be unable to get on the step. In that case, taxi in circles to make waves and try again right through the disturbance. Often this maneuver is enough to lift you through the hump.

If the lake is small and you need to get airborne with the shortest possible run, make a U-shaped takeoff. Get on the step downwind and make a 180-degree turn into the wind as close as possible to the lee shore. Often, it will halve the length of the upwind leg.

If light, low-powered floatplanes refuse to "unstick," when you are nearly up to takeoff speed, try rolling them with ailerons while holding course, so that one float lifts free of the water. This nearly halves the water resistance because the increased load on the remaining waterborne float adds little water drag at high taxi speed.

Often, takeoffs will be made from open water in temperatures below freezing. The airplane and windshields may ice up. Freshwater ice is hard. Saltwater ice remains mushy down to 22 or 20 degrees. Usually the accumulation will sublimate fairly soon after takeoff. However, it will greatly decrease the lift coefficient when it adheres to the leading edges. Recognize that the stalling speed will be raised dangerously. Attain extra airspeed before liftoff and climb—and don't land until the ice has gone. Also, ice may freeze around the joints of the landing gear in the wheel wells. As soon as you are airborne, cycle the gear up and down several times to prevent webs of solid ice from jamming in the joints. I have never yet heard of takeoff spray jamming the free motion of control surfaces, but it might pay under severe conditions to deliberately flex these too.

HAZARDS

Probably the worst in-flight hazard is striking *high-tension lines.* You feel like a bird flying low up a beautiful river, and you can do so with full safety when you have spotted high line crossings on your flight chart or predetermined that there are none. Although most of them now have highly visible large warning balls, they are very hard to see if there are no balls, so watch out.

The Federal Aviation Administration rules for low flying are the same for seaplanes as they are for landplanes. We must fly above 1000 feet over cities or populated areas and over 500 feet vertically *or horizontally* of any group of people or moving vehicles (which includes boats on the water), *except when taking off or landing.* There is no altitude restriction over open water. These rules permit seaplanes to land almost anywhere subject to the normal decency of not being obnoxious. A few state and local ordinances have closed some lakes to seaplanes. Before visiting your lakeshore friends, ask them to inform you if, perchance, there are restrictions. Even when there are, a local property owner may telephone the police and secure permission for a single landing and takeoff.

You will never be injured by striking *underwater ledges,* but they can severely dent your ego and hurt your pocketbook. If you are in navigable waters, marine charts will help to keep you in deep water, but the scale is so small they cannot help in selecting a safe place to nose ashore. However, the shaded depth contours in shoal water, and your own experience, will give good clues on whether to expect outlying rocks or shelving mud bottom. You would not expect rocks off a sandy shore, but you should be on guard when the adjacent shore is rocky. Generally speaking, expect a long point of land gradually sloping into the water to be shallow for some distance off the point. If the shoreline is steep, chances are the water will be deep quite close to shore. Here, note the word "chances"! Nevertheless, common sense and a bit of experience and planning will protect you. When you fly away from the big cities (and you will) you'll be surprised how frequently you can see bottom through the clear water.

When landing in small harbors and lakes or rivers lined with hills and trees, watch out for wind gradients. We all know wind velocities decrease near the surface of runways. Friction with the ground slows down the flow. However, we are not used to landing behind hills or near stands of tall trees. Behind such screens there may be a sharp shear line with normal wind just above the obstacle and no wind below it. Such a condition often helps in a crosswind landing. But if the approach is made into a steady wind while descending into the calm area, you will suddenly lose a lot of lift, possibly resulting in a full stall. Maintain plenty of reserve speed in the approach, and be ready with the throttle. I once had to use half of a good speed-reserve right in our own harbor, and the resulting engine roar required a round of visits to neighbors to apologize.

There may be minor hazards built right into your airplane. All floatplanes should have doors on *both* sides of the cabin. There should be clear and fast exit to either float. When there is only one door, the compromises that have to be made in docking or mooring are a very real hazard.

When you are leaving the dock and casting off a handling line, it may slide out the wing leading edge. If it meets at the tip with an extended Pitot tube and snarls, the ship may be yanked back into the dock in a swerving turn just as you gun it for a turn away.

All seaplanes should have water rudders. They have been omitted on a number of large twin-engine flying boats, the philosophy of the engineers being that the engines provided a more powerful steering force. The trouble is that force is unavailable just when you are cautiously approaching a dock and need the most accurate steering. Quite likely owners have paid more in insurance rates over the years than they would have paid to have special water rudders installed. Rudders must become standard.

When you are alone aboard, at a mooring, how do you climb back after you have fallen overboard? It is easy to climb the deck of a float, and the door of a very small flying boat with low freeboard. On large boats, better hand the boarding ladder out the door, even if you don't think you'll need it.

BASES

The layout plan and the facilities of seaplane bases vary too widely to categorize. Bases are marked on flight charts by an anchor inside a circle. Most bases include a ramp, apron with fuel pump, car parking area, hangar, and associated small buildings, with always a small outboard in attendance. Many, like the Twenty-third Street base in New York's East River, provide low floats, one with a fuel pump, and located out from the shore enough to permit approaches from three sides. The floats are deliberately narrow, so that a wing-tip float can be lifted over, permitting the hull to be made fast alongside. Many small boat marinas have seaplane facilities that rarely become noted on flight charts. A dock, fuel pump, attendants, and small-boat service to adjacent moorings are available at most marinas. Often they fly a wind sock, but few water pilots need one.

When Pan American operated big boats they placed a mooring just off the dock. When the plane was fast to the mooring, lines were led out from the dock by launches, and the big airplane was brought in to the debarking dock under firm restraint.

Naval flying boat bases have ramps and large-wheeled handling dollies permitting the large seaplanes to be brought ashore. Sometimes beaching gears are used. These are small wheels attached with struts to fittings on the side of the hull by a crew in waders. They are only strong enough to permit moving the plane around on aprons under tow. In remote bases, the Navy serviced flying boats from a good-sized vessel known as a seaplane tender. The seaplanes nosed into a bow-retaining float, positioned at the vessel's stern, permitting loading, fueling, and minor engine and maintenance work. Otherwise, seaplanes rode at moorings.

DAILY MAINTENANCE

Seaplanes require the same periodic maintenance and inspection as landplanes in regard to engines, controls, landing gear (amphib), instruments, and radios. Daily maintenance, however, is more important if based on salt water. Then the ship must be kept *clean* and free of salt deposits, especially in corners and around fittings. In temperate climates, corrosive action is very slow. In the warm and humid atmosphere of the tropics, prevention of corrosion requires cleaning almost daily. Seaplanes operating in freshwater lakes suffer little more than a landplane staked in the rain, except that interior steel parts may rust a bit faster if not protected.

Washing is best done with a hose spray. Unless the atmosphere is dirty and polluted, soap and scrubbing are rarely needed. It is enough that a freshwater spray is directed into all corners and crevices. There is no need to play the hose over the smooth sides. Corrosion is unlikely to occur on the outside aluminum surface, either bare or painted. The hose should be directed into all control surface hinges, all parts of an amphibian landing gear, and around external fittings. Flush out wheel pockets and brakes well, even lying down to direct the hose upward into wheel assemblies projecting through the bottom of amphibious floats. Remove the cowling and spray the engine with a mist of very light oil.

After a trip to the coast, most pilots land in the first freshwater lake they come to. Land roughly, taxi poorly, and thus souse the ship all over with spray and extend the landing gear for a few moments. Seagulls do it the same way! During the rainy season in the tropics, I used to fly with gear extended through the first rain shower on course. It's easier and faster than a hosing—and more thorough.

METAL PROPELLERS

Erosion, rather than corrosion, is the problem with metal propellers. Just as dirt and dents in the leading edge of a wing impair its efficiency, so does roughness on the leading edges of a propeller greatly spoil its thrust. Land plane props become severely roughened when flying through prolonged heavy rain, and smart pilots often lower the cruise RPM to reduce the erosion. On seaplanes, not only are spray droplets very large, but they strike the prop when it is at maximum RPM. If pits are not filed out when they are small, they will rapidly deepen and spread until ultimately the leading edge becomes almost split, with curved "horns" sticking out into the airflow.

It is a simple matter to dress the leading edges with a file when a little roughness first appears, but it takes a lot of hard work to remove real pits. Worse, severe filing may lead to unequal removal from opposite blades, throwing the propeller a little out of balance. "Honing," by rubbing the leading edges with a hardened steel bar a half-inch or more in diameter, is better than filing. It burnishes the aluminum and smooths by setting the surface back into shape rather than by removing material. However, any deep pit or nick should be filed and smoothed out carefully into the adjacent blade surface to prevent the propagation of cracks across the blade chord.

If this small effort sounds discouraging, remember that it is less trouble than removing nicks from propellers on tricycle landplanes operating from gravel runways. Flying stones are never mixed in flying spray!

CORROSION-PROOFING

Manufacturers of flying boats and hull-type amphibians corrosion-proof extensively during manufacture (see Chapter 20 under "Materials"). These are essential steps usually omitted in the manufacture of pure landplanes. All manufacturers will apply them on a special order basis at extra expense. It is more than worth it—it is essential. If you plan to purchase a used landplane with the intent of putting it on floats, make sure it was so prepared during original manufacture, unless you are willing to be confined only to freshwater operation.

OWNER'S PRECAUTIONS

Before putting your airplane into saltwater operation, it should be "greased." Every metal fitting, whether fixed or a moving part, should be coated with Par-el-ketone, Cosmoline, or equivalent. These are heavy thick greases usually brown in color. (Par-el-ketone is actually a form of lacquer.) They can be thinned and painted on fittings with a small brush. It also pays to unthread bolts and remove clevis pins, then reassemble after greasing the barrels. If this sounds irksome, you might be surprised how many purchasers of new outboard engines do the same before putting them into saltwater use. On both airplanes and outboards, it saves labor in the long run.

This attention should also be given to all control hinges and bell crank ends. However, care should be taken not to get the protective grease near prepacked ball bearings; the grease deteriorates their internal packing. Grease should also be applied to all moving parts of landing gears and water rudder mechanisms, door latches, fuel drains, etc. Exposed threads on tie rods and their clevises should be treated. Don't worry about the unpleasant brown color; it's worth it and barely shows, but do wipe the smears so that excess won't get on clothing as you brush by.

Cabins and luggage compartments should be kept clean and dry. This is not much of a problem on floatplanes, where the cabin is well above the water and muddy shoes first walk across float decks. It is a problem in small flying boats where the first step is onto the seat cushions. All dirt and moisture ultimately land on the inside bottom, where there is no escape by sweeping, and ventilation is often poor. Keep it clean. Lysol spray will prevent odors and mildew on upholstery.

A few spoonfuls of zinc-chromate crystals are often dropped into each compartment to mix with the residual bilge water that seems to be always present in small quantities, even after pumping. It forms a bright yellow liquid where your passengers won't see it, and inhibits corrosion in the places hardest to reach.

We will soon see *turbine engines* in commercial seaplanes. There are already turboprop "Twin Otters" on floats and a few turbine helicopters with pneumatic floats. Ingested salt spray causes encrustations on the turbine blades, inhibiting cooling and decreasing efficiency by altering their airfoil shape. Frequent cleaning is accomplished by spraying a freshwater or a light oil mist, or even ground walnut shells, directly into the intake before the engine is shut down.

Maintenance of *wooden* flying boats consists mostly of keeping them painted and well varnished. It is assumed that marine waterproof plywood is the basic material, and this deteriorates very slowly. *Fiberglass* hulls are probably the most durable of all—they just don't corrode. If they were made with a good original gel coating, they will need no painting for five or six years, but they should be waxed occasionally. Of course, the metal parts, fixed and moving, will need the same greasing attention as described for metal hulls. You may ask why fiberglass hulls are not more popular. Maybe they will be someday, but currently they are pretty heavy and not yet conducive to mass production.

Do not be afraid of corrosion. Many metal flying boats built before World War II are still flying happily after thirty or more years in saltwater operations. They undergo overhauls on the same schedule as landplanes. Piper Cubs on floats serve to spot schools of fish for the coastal work fleets. Many fathers and sons have flown the same ship over twenty years. We have seen Cubs off the coast under tow from trawlers, the last of a string of dories in a sea too rough for takeoffs. After living in salt water all summer, the family overhauls their plane in winter with few replacement parts or repairs.

When you apply the small attentions outlined in this chapter, fly happily off salt water and don't worry. You pay a bit for special proofing, and it takes a spot of work to keep corrosion under control, but that is a slight price to pay for seagoing wings. After a full summer of saltwater flying, most owners request a thorough professional inspection and cleaning, including paint touch-up. Even if it takes three men three days, the labor charges are less than the hangar rent would have been.

Buzz, a friend of ours, was hired to fly an unprepared seaplane one summer and was appalled at the extent of deterioration in the fall. No amount of explanation soothed his subsequent aversion to salt water, and we all kidded him unmercifully. He flew a fine twin-engine amphibian to California to demonstrate special equipment at Burbank, but forgot to lower the landing gear. In an attempt to cover his remorse, he sent the following telegram to New York:

Landed wheels up without damage. Repeat, no damage, except slight wear on keel at step. Please reply.

The reply was:

Buzz always avoided the ocean
To prevent salt water corrosion.
When landing, Burbank,
He forgot the wheel crank,
And suffered from runway erosion!

Be not afraid of corrosion!

U.S. SEAPLANE PILOTS ASSOCIATION

For further general information on seaplane operations, write

United States Seaplane Pilots Association
Little Ferry Seaplane Base
P.O. Box 13
Little Ferry, N.J. 07643

10

AMPHIBIAN BASICS

PERFORMANCE EFFICIENCY

Why do we lease, rent, or buy general aviation airplanes? Aside from the genuine fun of flying, it is basically for fast and convenient family utility or small-business transportation. Every pilot wistfully admires amphibian utility even before he has had a chance to experience it. How much does it cost and what performance can he expect in comparison to the landplane he knows?

The answers are involved in the illusive definition of "convenience." Some twenty-five years ago, many owners of small personal landplanes had thought how convenient it would be if they could fold their wings at the airport and drive into town, or drive the plane home and push it into the family garage. When weather forced down a non-instrument-rated pilot, he would fold the wings, drive over the mountains, and resume flying when he again found flyable weather. Their wistful dreams were very vivid, and many magazine articles extolled the idea.

At least four good aeronautical engineers tackled the problem. They produced and tested cleverly designed roadable airplanes. Two could detach the wings at the airport and drive the fuselage-engine-car unit into town. One folded the wings back, secured them to the tail, clutched the engine to the wheels, and drove off in the complete airplane. The fourth detached the wings, nestled them on a small trailer, and towed them behind. None of these roadable airplanes ever found a market. Despite ingenious design, they were poor airplanes and punk automobiles as well.

My old friend Allen Bourdon used to say of any airplane, "The trouble is, they're just a damn compromise." Roadables were too much of a compromise. Amphibians are just about the maximum compromise that does find a market because they go further than any other airplane type in solving the convenience issue. If amphibians are the means to more convenience, how much more do they cost to buy? to operate? and how much sacrifice is there in performance?

The most popular size general aviation landplane usually carries four passengers and their baggage, and cruises about 160 mph with a 675-mile range. The desired useful load averages about 1450 pounds. With an empty weight of 1700 pounds, the gross weight runs about 3150 pounds, and some 250 horsepower is required to secure this general performance. If the airplane meets normal takeoff and climb performance, the power loading will be about 12 pounds per horsepower, and the wing loading will run about 18 pounds per square foot, the sum of which is 30 pounds "per," which is the accepted criterion for good utility airplane performance in this class.

To secure the same payload and performance, an amphibian flying boat with retractable landing gear and other weight increments will run about 350 pounds more than an equivalent landplane. The new gross weight becomes about 3500 pounds for the same useful load, an 11 percent increase. To keep wing loading and power loading the same, both wing area and horsepower will also increase about 11 percent. A 280-horsepower engine will be required. A slightly larger airplane results. Unless we choose a further increment in power, it will fly a bit slower, perhaps 10 mph less with reduction in range to 635 miles. Cost increase results from the 280-horsepower engine, the slightly larger air frame, and the extra manufacturing cost in making a corrosion-resistant, watertight fuselage. A fair estimate is 30 percent more than the comparable landplane. If that had been equipped to cost $30,000, the amphib would cost $39,000 in round figures, with perhaps a 15 percent increase in hourly operating cost. If this increase seems excessive, check back on the cost increment you and your owner friends undertake when you purchase a new airplane that is always bigger, more powerful, faster, and with more electronics. For that jump in cost, did you get a comparable increase in landplane utility? To determine this we must first analyze the increased convenience utility an amphibian buys.

OPERATING EFFICIENCY

Every trip by a landplane involves three stages: the drive from departure to airport; the flight; and the drive from airport to destination. In a busy life, we are concerned with the overall elapsed time from departure to objective. A standard method of comparing the efficiency of one vehicle against another—or even one type of vehicle against any other type—is to rate them by payload, divided by the power, multiplied by the overall speed, departure to destination. For aircraft efficiency rating, the load is measured in tons, the installed horsepower is used, and the cruising speed is in miles per hour (or knots, if you prefer). So the formula is:

$$\frac{\text{tons}}{\text{hp}} \times \text{mph}, \quad \text{or,} \quad \frac{\text{tons}}{\text{hp}} \times \frac{\text{miles}}{\text{hours}},$$ for a trip of finite length.

But do not forget the first and third stages. When we add the time for these starting and finishing stages, we can compare the so-called "convenience efficiency" with full allowance for the moderately slower speed and greater power of the amphibian. Since fuel weight is a part of useful load, we will take the payload as a half ton for four people and baggage.

For years a Wall Street businessman commuted from a small lake near Rhinebeck, New York to a small float between two Hudson River piers, an 80-mile trip. We can analyze how much time the sample amphibian saves against the equivalent landplane and also work out the operating efficiencies of each. The following arithmetic shows he saved 50 minutes over the landplane and the efficiency is 75 percent greater. The same trip by automobile into New York traffic took nearly 2.5 hours.

Rhinebeck Lake to Hudson Pier: 80 miles

By landplane

1) :30—Home to airport
2) :30—Flight
3) :45—Airport to downtown

:105 = 1:45 = 1.75 hrs.

$$\frac{.5}{250} \times \frac{80}{1.75} = .091$$

By amphib

1) :05—On lake
2) :35—Flight
3) :15—Taxi to office

:55 = .9 hrs. (saved :50)

$$\frac{.5}{280} \times \frac{80}{.9} = .160$$ or 75 percent more efficient

Suppose on Friday afternoon he is going to spend a weekend with friends in Chatham on Cape Cod, 200 miles away. His amphibian is at Twenty-third Street seaplane base; his landplane is at one of the New York airports, probably Teterboro. This arithmetic shows he saves 45 minutes with 30 percent superior efficiency.

23rd St. to Chatham, Cape Cod: 200 miles

By landplane

1) :45—Office to airport
2) 1:15—Flight to Hyannis
3) :25—20 miles to Chatham

1:85 = 2:25 = 2.4 hrs.

$$\frac{.5}{250} \times \frac{200}{2.4} = .167$$

By amphib

1) :15—Taxi office to 23rd St.
2) 1:20—Flight
3) :05—On shore

1:40 = 1.67 hrs. (saved :45)

$$\frac{.5}{280} \times \frac{200}{1.67} = 2.16 \text{ or 30 percent more efficient}$$

Of course, the longer the trip, the less time the slightly slower amphibian saves. If he had flown 360 miles to popular Northeast Harbor on Mount Desert Island, Maine, or to the Bar Harbor Airport with his landplane, the arithmetic shows he still saves 40 minutes, though the efficiency is now only 10 percent better.

23rd St. to Northeast Harbor, Mount Desert Island, Maine: 360 miles

By landplane

1) :45—Office to airport
2) 2:15—Flight to Bar Harbor Airport
3) :25—20 miles to Northeast Harbor

2:85 = 3:25 = 3.4 hrs.

$$\frac{.5}{250} \times \frac{360}{3.4} = .212$$

By amphib

1) :15—Taxi office to 23rd St.
2) 2:25—Flight
3) :05—On shore

2:45 = 2.75 (saved :40)

$$\frac{.5}{280} \times \frac{360}{2.75} = .235 \text{ or 10 percent more efficient}$$

We don't use airplanes just for time efficiency. With his amphibian anchored in front of his friends' cottage, he probably took them out to fish from the plane, or to get lobsters right from the lobsterman's smack, or to check on how their kids were doing in the yacht club race. The next day he may have flown them up to beautiful Moosehead

Lake for a Sunday picnic. His amphibian is giving him "convenience utility," and the time of his life, too. The landplane, you may be sure, would have remained on the airport all weekend.

Amphibians offer many secondary economies. When there is less ground transportation needed, there is less taxi and car rental cost. Compared with pure seaplanes, say on a vacation trip, all enroute airport facilities are the same as for landplanes. Refueling, weather information, and lunch at airports are immediate. Amphibians will take you direct on a camping trip to a remote Canadian lake without the cost of hiring a local floatplane to take you in. Departure is at your convenience without waiting for the scheduled seaplane pickup. If you're flying the continent by landplane, you will probably choose overnight stops at airports with motels—and listen to the other airplanes roar all night. By amphibian, you pick the scenic motels on lakes, away from commercialism, probably with your plane at anchor in sight of the breakfast table. The midcontinent Ozark Mountain recreation area has many fine lakeside hotels.

Fortunately, today forced landings in single-engine airplanes are pretty rare, but when they do occur the amphibian pilot has the best chance of accomplishing an off-airport landing gracefully. If he is forced down by weather, he will not have to fly long, except perhaps in the far West, before he will find a bit of water to receive him.

WHEEL POSITION INDICATORS

Many devices have been patented and used for a short while to assure the pilot he will select the correct landing gear position in an airplane that lands half the time on water and half the time on land. Lights, horns, even bells have been inserted in electric circuits that you preset for the anticipated wheel position you will next require—if you remember to preset—or even if you know ahead on what surface you will land—if you don't change your mind! It gets complicated.

When the landing gear operating lever is in the instrument board and not at the side of the seat, indicator lights incorporated right in the lever assembly are preferred. Time has shown the best method is to school yourself to say *out loud* when you start an approach, "I am landing on water and my wheels are *up*" or "I am landing on land and my wheels are *down*." And again, *repeat it aloud* and *look* at the indicator before the landing flare is started. Don't be embarrassed about it. Say it aloud thoughtfully and deliberately on *every* landing. No automatic mechanical system can do better.

For years the Loening Aircraft Company delivered amphibians from their factory located in the heart of New York City with a ramp out the back door on the East River. The story is told of an Army pilot who came to take delivery of a new Loening and went out with the factory pilot for the usual familiarization flight. After shooting landings on water, they went over to Roosevelt Field to practice landings on land. On every approach the check pilot had to remind the Army man to lower his wheels before landing. The Army pilot was badly shaken. Upon returning to New York, the high buildings passing his wing tip and the bridges overhead rattled him even more. With teeth clenched he remembered to lower the wheels and approach the river, only to be again reminded this time they should be up! As soon as the ship settled off the step, he stepped out of the cockpit, shaking his head in self-disgust, and stepped off the trailing edge, as he would on land—and fell into the river!

PART TWO

Seaplane Development: *History, Current Design, Future*

11

NATIONALISTIC DEVELOPMENT

As soon as the Wright Brothers achieved the first successful powered flight on 17 December 1903, the great nations of the world plunged helter-skelter into exploitation of man's long cherished dream of wings. Nations and their citizens as individuals, and their military, vied with each other to fly even better. Each new idea was immediately copied and improved. Aircraft somewhat alike, yet nationally individualistic, perfectly reflected the national character of each country. One could almost look at a picture of a new airplane and determine the originating nation.

A little over six years after the Wright brothers' flight in December 1903, Henri Fabre of France made the first successful flight from water in March 1910. His remarkably light and ingenious seaplane achieved its first flight from the water, unlike most of its successors which flew first as landplanes. It would be classified today as a tailfirst pusher. Powered with a Gnome engine, the "fuselage" was merely a light stick beam with the elevator controls on the forward end. The pilot sat astride the upper rail. There were one forward and two after floats in somewhat the same con-

March 28, 1910 on the French Riviera—Henri Fabre makes the first seaplane flight. (Musee de l'Air)

figuration as a modern front-steering iceboat. The floats were small and approximately square in shape with flat bottoms and cambered upper surfaces. It appears to have flown well under good control right from the start. But after attaining success, nothing more was heard of the Fabre seaplane.

For the next twenty years, seaplanes led landplanes in advancing design and performance. Development skyrocketed. Effective military seaplanes appeared in World War I. Serious civil use of seaplanes followed. The history of seaplane operations is well described in Edward Jablonski's recent book *Sea Wings*, published by Doubleday. The history of technical progress is equally exciting.

The next successful seaplane designer was Glenn Curtiss at Hammondsport, New York, who soon transferred his base to North Island in San Diego, California, which became a major US naval air base. Curtiss had already been working on seaplane design at the time of the Fabre flight. After trying unsuccessfully thirty varied configurations, even mounting a Curtiss landplane on a canoe hull, he finally flew off the water in January 1911, using a central float with a flat bottom of square cross section and without a step. His seaplane was stabilized laterally by single inclined planks at the wing tips. The US Navy showed immediate attention, placing an order for an improved version, which Curtiss delivered in July that same year! Also later that year, Curtiss added wheels to the float and made the first successful amphibian flights.

In January 1912, Curtiss delivered the first real flying boat, in which the pilot sat inside a streamline lightweight hull. This aircraft still supported the tail on outriggers, but

January 21, 1914—Curtiss OWL-1 "Over Water Land," the first amphibian. (Virville Collection, National Air and Space Museum)

Curtiss MF Seagull with Hisso engine. A great barnstormer from the beaches.

soon tails were mounted directly on the stern of the hull, thus inaugurating the famous long run of Curtiss F flying boats. Later they became MFs and finally, during the twenties, the ubiquitous four-passenger Seagull.

Curtiss's success inspired many others. Grover Loening, the first graduate aeronautical engineer, then working with the Wright brothers, produced a seaplane version of the Wright Flyer in 1913. Only a year later, the first regular scheduled airline in the world started flights between St. Petersburg and Tampa, Florida, using Benoist flying boats. Starling Burgess and a host of others on both sides of the Atlantic quickly designed and flew their seaplanes. Flying boats captured public fancy and confidence, perhaps because they preceded landplanes with enclosed fuselages. Pilot and passengers sat inside, giving the craft the appearance and operating environment of familiar small surface boats.

Many weekends in the twenties I barnstormed in Curtiss Jenny landplanes, hunting up a suitable field alongside a

1914—the world's first scheduled airline: Benoist flying boat at Tampa, Florida. (Smithsonian Institution)

road. People driving by would watch but were very reluctant to buy a flight. On two Sundays I barnstormed a Seagull from Revere Beach, Boston. What a difference! The Seagull brought aviation to the people in a more or less familiar-looking craft. We had many more customers than dared to fly in the awkward-looking landplanes.

In 1913, the London *Daily Mail* offered a $50,000 prize for the first successful flight across the North Atlantic. The prize inspired Glenn Curtiss to build a very large flying boat powered with two OX–5 pusher engines. The three-man crew was housed inside a relatively comfortable enclosed cabin. It is doubtful if this airplane, named the *America*, could ever have flown the ocean, even though a third engine was later mounted on the upper wing. However, it looked businesslike and greatly spurred the subsequent growth of larger, more capable flying boats.

The *America* led at once to the Curtiss H series of twin-engine Navy flying boats. Only four months after World

War I started, Curtiss delivered two of the H–4s to Great Britain, which immediately copied and rapidly improved them for naval coastal patrol reconnaissance, as Porte and Felixstowe boats with Rolls–Royce engines. The United States continued development of the H series with Liberty engines. Somewhere in the program, the engines changed from pusher propellers to tractor propellers. The American H–16s were nearly comparable to the F–5–Ls which came back to us from England. I flew one for a few hours six years after the war. At that time she seemed huge, but was great fun to fly.

The famous NC series of flying boats was designed during the war. These were powered with four Liberty engines, three tractor and one pusher. The tail was carried on giant outriggers. Becoming operational just at the end of the war, they accomplished the famous first crossing of the Atlantic Ocean in May 1919, slightly less than five years after the *America* had flown.

Curtiss H-16 with Liberty engines—W.W.I patrol plane. (US Navy)

First to fly the Atlantic: the NC-4 landing at Lisbon, Portugal, May 1919. (Smithsonian Institution)

This flight inaugurated many innovations in international competition. Not counting Blériot's first flight across the English Channel, it initiated the first flight between nations that were previously separated and protected from invasion and aggression by the deep seas. It was the first group flight. Four planes started, though only the NC–4 arrived in England. It was the first military-financed flight. It "showed the flag" to establish national prestige. It presaged the many American exploration flights that were later to lead the world in aerial explorations.

Great Britain, always a maritime nation, took the lead in developing large flying boats throughout the twenties and early thirties. Unfortunately, she adhered too long to the slow biplane. Only in the late thirties did she produce faster,

Short Empire used on the long London-to-Melbourne, Australia route. (Smithsonian Institution)

Saunders Roe Cutty Sark amphibian. (Smithsonian Institution)

longer-range monoplanes, culminating in the Royal Navy Sunderlands and the civil Empires. Few floatplanes appeared in England during this period, though she produced a wide variety of smaller military and commercial flying boats.

France continued to develop seaplanes, mostly in small sizes, until the period of transatlantic passenger flying was imminent. Then she produced several large flying boats that might have gone into production had not the holocaust of World War II interrupted.

In the twenties, Germany designed a few superior seaplanes, both large and small. Lacking national airlines, even to neighboring countries, none attained large production. By the midthirties Germany's economy was thriving again. There were no longer Allied peace limitations on her merchant marine, and now her fast passenger vessels were

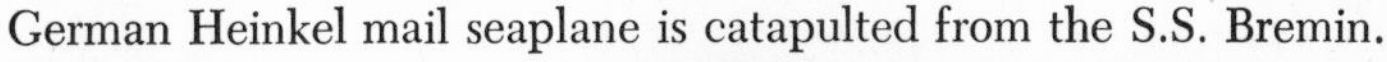
German Heinkel mail seaplane is catapulted from the S.S. Bremin.

supreme in the North and South Atlantic. She sought to accelerate mail delivery between the continents. Catapults were installed on her crack steamers, permitting single-engine Heinkel and four-engine Blohm and Vass floatplanes to be launched as soon as the vessels came within flying range of port. The system often saved two days in ocean mail delivery.

Italy has traditionally designed very sleek, beautiful landplanes. She also built many small, clean seaplanes, but strangely her international success came with an odd-appearing type, the Savoia–Marchetti twin-hull flying boat. Commander Francisco de Pinedo embarked on a brilliant series of long-range flights in one of these aircraft. Flying to Tokyo and back, he later crossed the South Atlantic and made a grand tour of the United States before returning home. A few years later, Commander Italo Balbo flew the

Savoia-Marchetti S-55P: the only catamaran flying boat, but a champion for her day. (Smithsonian Institution)

Bourdon-Viking Kitty Hawk—designed by the author. (Leighton Collins)

Douglas World Cruiser—first around the world, but half the flights were made as a landplane. (McDonnell Douglas Company)

flag of Fascist Italy in a series of "Armada" flights, a squadron of fourteen flying in formation. After a round trip to Buenos Aires, he flew across the North Atlantic to attend the Chicago World's Fair and appear in many other American cities.

In the United States, development proceeded and expanded on all types of seaplanes for all civil and military missions. Increasing passenger capacity and range of both pure flying boats and amphibians soon led to airline service to South America. Unlike those of other countries, nearly all successful American types won relatively large domestic and export production orders. For several decades, the Edo Aircraft Corporation held a monopoly on the manufacture of aluminum twin floats which converted most of the popular utility and privately owned landplane types into very excellent floatplanes. The company prospered on orders for pleasure flying and business use, particularly in Canada. Although the prices were high, the excellence of Edo floats stifled competition for years.

World exploration by seaplane became the United States' contribution to history during this period. There were many "good-will" flights into friendly countries and the world's more inaccessible areas. The Navy, the Army, and many civilians participated. Nineteen twenty-four saw the completion of the first flight around the world, accomplished by four Army Douglas specially designed World Cruisers. They were large biplanes powered with single Liberty engines and easily converted from landplanes to twin-float seaplanes. Making the 26,345-mile flight in many stages, they flew Seattle to Seattle in 175 days. About half the stages were as seaplanes and half as landplanes. Two craft were wrecked and replaced by others for the final triumphal flight across the United States.

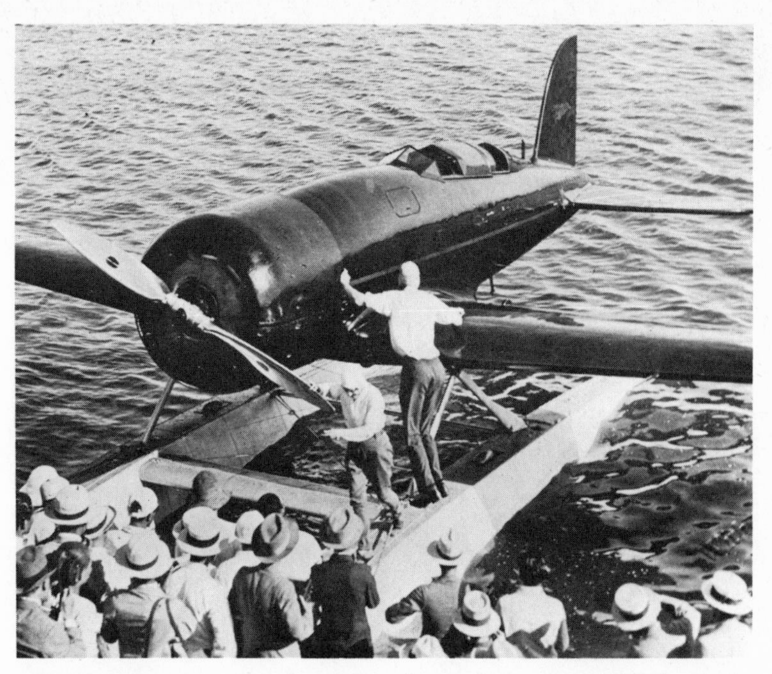

Lockheed Serius with Colonel Charles and Anne Lindbergh. (Edo Aircraft)

The Army next flew brilliant good-will flights all around South America in a group of four Loening amphibians. In the midtwenties, small American seaplanes had explored the entire length of the Amazon River and all of Canada, penetrating north to the Arctic Circle. In the early thirties, Admiral Richard E. Byrd flew over the North and South Poles in landplanes, but he also flew a Curtiss Condor biplane transport on large twin floats to explore the shores of Antarctica.

In 1931, Colonel Charles Lindbergh and his wife, Anne, explored the northern route to Japan by way of Alaska and the Aleutians. Their plane was a long range Lockheed low-wing Sirius twin-float seaplane. Next they made an even more useful exploratory flight for Pan American Airways, all around the North and South Atlantic by way of Labrador, Greenland, Iceland, Europe, the Azores, Africa, South America, and home. This famous seaplane was retired after 37,000 miles of exploratory flight.

Seaplane exploration of the dark corners of the world still continues, but the effective termination of these enterprises occurred on August 15, 1935, aviation's saddest day. Beloved Will Rogers and the great pilot Wiley Post were killed on a good-will flight to the Orient in the crash of their plane, similar to the Lindbergh's, near Point Barrow, Alaska.

12

BETWEEN THE WARS

Did you have trouble distinguishing a Boeing 707 from a Douglas DC–8 or a Convair 990? Or do you now confuse a Douglas DC–10 and a Lockheed L–1011? It is surprising how the advancement of research and design art in recent years has produced aircraft so much alike. It was not so in the rapid development of flying boats in this period. Each company had a distinct design concept or formula by which their products were universally recognized. In the United States at least five major companies developed a series of new designs so distinctive that any interested schoolboy could instantly identify the manufacturer when he first saw a photograph of each new aircraft.

LOENING

Grover Loening was a leader in seaplane design. In the early twenties, his Air Yacht monoplane powered with a pusher Liberty engine captured many world's performance records and won commercial orders. The military, however, still specified biplane types, leading to the famous Loening Amphibian. Looking like a conventional landplane, except that the fuselage was extremely deep to form a hull, it was powered with an inverted Liberty engine running "upside down." The bow extended forward under the raised propeller, looking like a large shoe. The wheels folded into pockets on the side of the hull. As more powerful radial engines became available, this distinctive design grew in size until the engine was raised to the leading edge of the upper wing above a large passenger cabin while still retaining the basic Loening concept.

Boeing, Ireland, and others made single-engine pusher flying boat biplanes, but Douglas and American Fokker, later North American and now Rockwell International Corporation, led the way to clean cantilever monoplanes in this country. They mounted the wing on top of the hull with the pilot sitting forward. Both had twin engines in nacelles. The Fokker Antares used them as pushers. The Douglas nacelles were tractors installed above and ahead of the leading edge.

Loening Amphibian ordered by the Army, Navy and Coast Guard for its unique adaptable utility. (US Coast Guard)

Thurston Flying Boat with retractable hydrofoil. (Thurston Aircraft)

Griswold Polyphibian taxiing on water ski. (Roger Griswold)

Douglas Dolphin Amphibian with two P. & W. Wasp engines. (US Coast Guard)

MARTIN—CONSOLIDATED

Until 1928, the Navy designed and manufactured its own patrol biplanes with two tractor engines in nacelles between the wings. The Martin PN series looked much the same. The Consolidated Aircraft Company of San Diego, which be-

Consolidated Commodore. Navy patrol biplanes lead to airline types and become monoplanes. (General Dynamics)

came Consolidated–Vultee and later the Convair Division of General Dynamics, broke away from biplanes with an intermediate "sesqui-plane" using a very short lower wing to brace the upper wing and support close-in tip floats. Their P2Y Navy patrol was a pure monoplane and quickly became their first commercial boat, the Commodore, carrying twenty passengers. Their hulls retained distinctive lines carrying into the famous PBYs.

SIKORSKY

Igor I. Sikorsky produced his first airplane in Czarist Russia before World War I. He was the first to develop large twin- and multi-engine aircraft. Having no sympathy with the Bolshevik Revolution, he migrated to the United States in the early twenties and produced a brilliant forerunner of passenger land transports to come. Then, with the help of his Russian friends, he established his own company, soon transferring from Long Island to a fine new aircraft factory in Bridgeport, Connecticut.

As a designer, Sikorsky thought first in terms of structure and light weight. His early seaplanes were considered homely, almost ungainly. They were distinctive indeed, featuring external struts, outrigger tails, and other drag-producing excrescences, but they were structurally light and

Sikorsky S-38 Amphibian in Army colors, though she won more renown commercially.

carried good payloads. They were also amphibians and had an instant sales appeal at a time when speed was relatively unimportant because airplane speed so far exceeded any steamship speed. On the Caribbean run to South America frequent refueling stops in sheltered harbors caused little delay. Juan Trippe early recognized their worth and became Sikorsky's largest customer. With these planes he launched Pan American Airways, for whom Charles Lindbergh became a consultant, piloting many of their pioneering runs.

GRUMMAN

The Grumman Aircraft Engineering Corporation started business in 1929 manufacturing amphibious floats for attachment under Navy landplanes. Not long after, they produced the Grumman Duck, a single-engine biplane amphibian along

Grumman G-21 Goose. Basically commercial, it became a JRF-5 in Navy, Army, or Coast Guard use. (US Coast Guard)

Grumman G-44 Widgeon. Mr. Leroy Grumman said, "The Coast Guard is not our largest customer. It is just our best customer." (US Coast Guard)

the lines of the former Loening but now more modern in appearance. Below the fuselage, but attached permanently to it at all times, there was a hull resembling an amphibian float. These models were built through the thirties and into World War II.

In 1936, Grumman first flew the Goose, a compact eight-passenger commercial type with two Wasp Junior engines. It featured very high performance and again sponsored a

Grumman JF2 Duck Amphibian coming aboard a vessel. Note the padded "V" rods waiting to fend off, which were essential when the vessel was rolling. (US Coast Guard)

distinctive long line of other typically Grumman twin-engines. Now, like fast landplanes, cowled engines were faired into the wing leading edge. The smaller Widgeon first flew in 1939 with Ranger engines and carried five people. The Navy and Air Force commandeered all these aircraft at the start of World War II, and Grumman continued their manufacture, using the existing tooling to capacity for Navy utility missions. Of all the aircraft I ever flew, the little Widgeon was my favorite.

DORNIER

The Dornier Aircraft Company, located on Lake Constance, Germany, designed and manufactured its own long series of distinctive and capable seagoing boats, starting with the six-passenger, single-engine Delphine and going on to multiple-engine craft, with a variety of engine locations but all of the basic Dornier appearance. The hallmark of Dornier boats was the seawings, or sponsons, which replaced conventional outboard floats. The German government and Dornier had their eyes set from the outset on future transatlantic passenger service. As early as 1920 they floated the first of the world's giant flying boats described in the next chapter. In the late 1930s, the long development line reached the DO–36, a four-engine, very clean flying boat, which used retractable wing-tip floats, the first time for Dornier. It was very successfully used in both northern and southern transatlantic crossings purely as a mail plane.

GREAT BRITAIN

True to her marine heritage, England excelled in flying boats. For two decades, intense rivalry prevailed between

Short Kent, which started regular service to Great Britain's distant colonies. (Flight International)

The Piggy Back solution to first transatlantic mail. (Imperial Airways)

the firms of Short, Sopwith, Vickers, Saunders–Roe, Blackburn, and Supermarine. These flying boats, for many years, were ever larger biplanes, and although they had a forest of struts, they were rugged and capable in rough-water landings, superior to those of other countries. Unfortunately, their "built-in headwinds" resulted in low speed and, therefore, relatively short range.

Britain was most interested in establishing mail and passenger service to her distant colonies. In the late twenties, she had regular service to Malta and the Mediterranean, and by 1932 the giant Short Kent four-engined class serviced Africa, the Near East, India, Singapore, Hong Kong, and Australia. From the point of view of passenger miles flown, England led all other nations.

Unfortunately, she did not abandon biplanes early enough. The first monoplane flying boats were the short Canopus series in 1936. They were capable, faster, and longer ranged, but still behind the new American flying boat achievements. Toward the end of the thirties, England did capture honors in long-range mail delivery with a unique Piggy Back aircraft. A very fast, small, four-engine, twin-float seaplane called the Mercury was mounted by crane above a Short Empire boat. This composite provided wing area and, more important, eight-engine thrust, to get the overloaded combination into the air. After a short outbound flight, the Mercury would detach, speed up, and continue on its own, while the mother plane returned to base. Transatlantic mail flights to Montreal and regular service to the Mediterranean continued through the year before World War II began.

UNITED STATES FLOATPLANES

In addition to the growing interest in long-range patrol boats, the US Navy continued with small single-float seaplanes made by Curtiss and Vought. Shipboard scouts were hoisted overboard at sea and took off in the relatively smooth slick produced by the vessel's slow turn out of the wind. A similar maneuver permitted landing in seas otherwise too rough. They were retrieved by a crane with some hazard and occasional damage. An improvised ramp towed slowly at the stern of the cruiser proved a little better. A platform of tough fabric encircling a horizontal spar at the waterline made a yielding taut ramp. The little seaplanes taxied onto this ramp and were hoisted aboard by a stern-mounted crane. The Navy lost interest in floatplanes in the early thirties. Thereafter, reconnaissance and torpedo-carrying landplanes were carrier borne.

Nevertheless, scout floatplanes were aboard US Navy cruisers, particularly when in foreign ports, right up to our entry into World War II. Just at the time Paris fell to the

Vought OS2U-3, one of the last of the many US Navy single float seaplanes. (US Coast Guard)

Germans, I was in Lisbon for the purpose of assembling Grumman flying boats and checking out the Portuguese pilots. These twelve were the only pure boats Grumman ever built. There had been a movement afoot in Portugal to combine the Army and Navy flying forces, much to the distaste of the Navy pilots, who believed they should be a part of the seagoing fleet. Hence, they ordered the Grummans as pure flying boats. Not only was the landing gear omitted, but the inside fittings and structure to which it attached were eliminated during manufacture. Since they could not possibly be based at an Army airport, the merger proposal was dropped.

While we were assembling the first ship, the US Navy cruiser *Trenton* anchored in the Tagus River. Daily at noon, when half of Lisbon came down to the Prado for lunch, the *Trenton*'s two floatplanes were lowered over the side and flew sedately up and down the river for a half hour. When the day came for the first flight, I suggested to the captain of the Bon Success Naval Base that we take off shortly before noon, and if all was well with the ship, we, too, might fly by the Prado. With an understanding smile, he said he would fly with me. Taking off down the river away from the city, we flew low almost behind the olive trees far south of the city and circled about ten miles upriver until we saw the two scouts go overboard. Using their first circle to time our arrival, we climbed until they were again ready to fly low past the waterfront, and came down in a screaming 220-mile-per-hour dive, passing between them and the Prado.

The Portuguese Navy had withheld publicity on their new fleet, and our appearance was a complete surprise. The floatplanes flying at less than half our speed looked as if they were going to spin in. The Grumman banked away from the city, revealing to all Lisbon the identifying marks painted under the wings—the ancient Portuguese sailing crosses long borne by Portuguese vessels, which had become the identifying mark of their military aircraft. And, of course, we flew circles around the scouts until they landed. The following Sunday I was the guest of the ranking admiral for an all-day tour of the Castle of Sintra and other landmarks. A few days later, I attended a welcoming function to the US Navy visiting officers where I met the captain of the *Trenton*. There were no hard feelings—there never were among pilots.

THE SCHNEIDER TROPHY RACES

While seaplanes were leading the way to larger and heavier airplanes, they were also leading in the quest for more speed. The almost annual Schneider Trophy Races were open to entries from any country, though all but a scattering came from England, France, Italy, and the United States. Starting in 1913, they continued almost every year until 1931, terminating only when the developments they pioneered were applied to landplanes. By that time landplanes were at last adopting retractable landing gears and so became faster than equivalent seaplanes. Landplanes thereafter held the world's speed records.

Usually the winning Schneider seaplane was the one with the most powerful engine. The contests were the proving ground for engine development, not perhaps in engine weight, but rather in reducing engine bulk. The last air-cooled winner was in 1920. Thereafter, the lead toward more power and less drag was taken by in-line water-cooled engines. The races took immediate advantage of every propeller development, including thin metal blades and controllable pitch.

Sleek streamlining was essential. When metal construction replaced wood, the racers demanded smoother skins and

Sopwith Tabloid—1914 Schneider Trophy winner. (Smithsonian Institution)

Supermarine S-6B—1931 and last Schneider Trophy winner at 340 miles per hour. (Flight International)

pioneered flush riveting. Engine-cooling drag was a big problem. Bulky water radiators were replaced by thin flush-skin wing-surface radiators, still further advancing the art of metal construction. The Supermarine S–6B, the last winner, even had flush radiators in the floats. However, skin radiators were not adopted by other airplanes because of vulnerability to gunfire and because water-cooled engines were by then yielding to air cooling.

As indicated in the following table, biplanes yielded to monoplanes and flying boats gave way to twin-float seaplanes. The final winner, the Supermarine S–6B, was the direct parent of the famous Supermarine Spitfire that won the Battle of Britain ten years later.

Year	*Seaplane*	*Speed in mph*	*Configuration*
1913	Deperdussin	75	Monoplane
1914	Sopwith	78	Biplane—twin float
1919	Savoia	?	Biplane—boat (Disqualified)
1920	Savoia S–13	102	Biplane—boat
1921	Macchi VII	118	Biplane—boat
1922	Supermarine Sea Lion	147	Biplane—boat
1923	Curtiss Navy Racer	173	Biplane—twin float
1925	Curtiss Army Racer	235	Biplane—twin float
1926	Macchi M–39	244	Monoplane—twin float
1927	Supermarine S–5	265	Monoplane—twin float
1929	Supermarine S–6	326	Monoplane—twin float
1931	Supermarine S–6B	340	Monoplane—twin float

In those eighteen years, speed increased 450 percent, or 25 percent per year. The limiting speed for propeller-driven aircraft is about 450 mph. The introduction of jet engines after World War II, and the attainment of supersonic flight, boosted maximum speed at extreme altitudes to nearly 2000 mph, an increase of another 450 percent. However, this advance required twenty-seven years, increasing only 16 percent per year. It is hard to believe that greater advances occurred in those years than aviation can achieve today.

One of the most interesting seaplanes of all time, the Macchi P.C. VII, was prepared for the 1931 contest, which proved to be the last. When desperate testing failed to make the deadline of that race, further development was canceled just before she almost flew. Two powerful water-cooled engines in tandem gave her twice the power of her would-be competitors with no increase in fuselage width. They drove a propeller in the nose, but also drove a water propeller under the tail, which would be feathered in flight. A pair of footlike hydrofoils substituted for twin floats and would surely have greatly reduced air drag. She floated on her streamlined watertight fuselage with the high wing just awash and the waterline only about ten inches below the open cockpit rim. There are photographs of her planing, tail low, on the hydrofoils with the air propeller well clear of the water. She is not the only promising airplane to go down in history as a failure when a little more expense probably would have made her a success.

13

THE NAVAL PATROL FLYING BOATS

By the midthirties, invaluable research data from the Langley Field Laboratory of the National Advisory Committee for Aeronautics (the NACA, forerunner of the NASA) gave the United States the recognized lead in all types of aircraft. The towing basin there, so long that the curvature of the earth could be measured on its surface, supplied a constant flow of information enabling designers to create ever more seaworthy hulls with faster takeoffs. These data, much more powerful engines, metal construction, and improved cantilever-wing design all combined to encourage the Navy to issue specifications for a new breed of patrol flying boats. Martin, Douglas, and Boeing submitted fine prototypes, but Consolidated beat them out because their boat was the first to fly in 1936 and had the longest potential range. The incomparable PBY, or Catalina, was born—the champion of World War II.

The Martin PBM Mariner flew a few years later and was also delivered in goodly numbers during the war, both to the United States Navy and England's Fleet Air Arm. Though her star was much less brilliant than the Catalina's, she led to the P3M and other Martin patrol planes delivered over an

The superb and well-loved Consolidated Catalina. (General Dynamics)

Martin Mariner PBM featured a "cranked" or gull-wing to raise the props. (Smithsonian Institution)

even longer period. This boat, with a distinctive "cranked" wing to get the props higher out of spray, had a top speed over 200 mph and a light-load ferry range of 3000 miles.

THE FAITHFUL CATALINAS

The PBY Catalina bore the stamp of Consolidated design. Her large unflapped wing of 104-foot span was lightly loaded. Nearly cantilever, it was mounted on a narrow central pylon high about the hull in which the engineer sat in noisy solitude. Her long, gracefully curved tail imparted a bushy appearance in accord with her eager, try-anything nature. She was the first to have retractable wing-tip floats, which formed a shrouded wing tip when fully raised. It was common practice to lift the floats early in the takeoff run as soon as lateral aileron control became effective. She enjoyed one of the longest production runs in history, lasting well into the 1950s. No one knows how many are still flying. Surely, a couple of dozen must be operating in the remote corners of the world even today. Occasionally, one will come up for resale in this country or Canada and be listed in Trade-A-Plane advertisements. At least one is still flying as a personal luxury yacht. Another is operated by Antilles Airlines in the Virgin Islands. It is sad they are dying out. Sadder still, I never had the opportunity to fly one of these superb aircraft!

"Pig boats," as they were sometimes affectionately called, were applied to a variety of Navy missions: patrol; torpedo plane; bomber; ASW (antisubmarine warfare); rescue; reconnaissance; convoy protection; glider tug (as amphibian); night bomber; and mail and freight transport.

SUNDERLANDS

The great British Short Sunderlands were first delivered to the Royal Navy on the eve of World War II. They continued in active service throughout the war and even beyond 1950. Matching the Catalina in missions and performance, these tough four-engined boats bristled with guns and depth charges. They were the nemesis of any submarine caught on the surface. They were perhaps the most seaworthy boats of all time, capable of operations into and out of extremely heavy seas. Both the Sunderland and Catalina were great rescue aircraft. When the seas were too rough for landing,

The great British Short Sunderland, which was superb in rough seas. (Smithsonian Institution)

they directed surface vessel help to downed pilots. When conditions permitted, they landed to effect the direct rescue themselves, using inflatable rafts to bring the pilots aboard.

It is interesting to compare the characteristics of the two aircraft.

	Catalina	*Sunderland*
Power	2 Pratt and Whitney 2400 hp	4 Rolls-Royce Pegasus 4000 hp
Span	104 ft.	112 ft.
Gross Weight	27,000 lbs.	45,000 lbs.
Cruising Speed	160 to 120 mph	175 mph
Range	4000 miles	3000 miles

These are only approximate figures, because under war conditions either would be loaded to the very maximum commensurate with the sea conditions and requirements of the mission. Two cruising speeds are listed for the Catalinas. Because of their light wing-loading, they secured long range by the ability to throttle down to 120 mph and reduce the fuel consumption. When fuel economy was not a consideration, they cruised nearly as fast as the Sunderlands on little more than half the horsepower.

WARTIME ACHIEVEMENTS

The little-known, far-ranging, overocean patrols flown by American Catalina and British Sunderland flying boats were an extremely important channel to victory during the war. Eighteen- or twenty-hour patrols, in cold, misty weather over raging seas that would tear a flying boat to bits if a landing were attempted, were devoid of glamour. Fatigue from long periods in cold, cramped positions, boredom, and rare success in sighting an enemy was undoubtedly the hardest lot of any of the wartime flight crews. Nevertheless, of all the outstanding, fine aircraft of the war, the lonely, almost forgotten Catalina must rank among the very first.

The United States was supporting the Allies by a vulnerable supply line of convoys, and marauding German submarines took a vicious toll. Subs were hunted and sunk from the air and from vessels at sea, but these were hardly combat operations; the submarines were ineffective in fighting back. The Germans desperately wanted to give them attacking support. When the pocket battleship *Bismarck* eluded the British fleet and escaped from the North Sea, she could effectively support undersea operations with the advantage of offensive attack. The great British surface navy could not protect all the convoys from such a fast raiding vessel. Great destruction to Allied shipping was threatened. As long as the

Bismarck was prowling the sealanes, Germany might well be able to launch her long-planned invasion of England.

On May 26, 1941, a Catalina, hundreds of miles west of Ireland, suddenly saw the threatening hull of the *Bismarck* speeding below, half obscured in the fog. Immediately, news of her location was radioed and the entire British fleet mobilized to kill the *Bismarck*. The discovering Catalina shadowed the *Bismarck*'s course until the last minute before compelled by diminishing fuel to turn back. Just then, the first relieving Catalina pulled up alongside, waves were exchanged, and the replacing Catalina continued following the *Bismarck*. In turn others came until the battle was joined and the brand new warship was sunk. It is interesting that the final *coup de grâce* was given by waves of extremely obsolete, slow, torpedo-dropping Swordfish biplanes.

A year later another patroling Catalina on dull patrol duty far out in the lonely Pacific had no inkling that a powerful Japanese fleet was headed again for Hawaii in the hope of administering a second and even more devastating blow to Pearl Harbor, which they planned to destroy after attacking Midway. Suddenly, below them, they found the extensive Japanese fleet. Once again a lowly Catalina sent the alarm and shadowed the fleet until relieved by other patroling Catalinas. Soon the battle of Midway was fought. The ensuing American victory turned the tide in the Pacific. No longer was there doubt of the eventual outcome. There was long, hard fighting to come, but from that day the doughty "Cats" assured victory in the Pacific. A slow-flying boat became one of the great airplanes of World War II.

POSTWAR PATROL FLYING BOATS

The Japanese also had a good long-range patrol boat, the Kawanishi 22, the Emily, powered by four Mitsubishi engines of 1825 horsepower each, grossing 68,000 pounds and spanning 124 feet. They had a 170-mile-per-hour cruising speed and a range of nearly 3000 miles, and closely resembled the Sunderland. However, their wartime effectiveness was severely curtailed by our surface and air operations.

The Martin P5M-2 Marlin was the follow-on from the Mariner. Designed more for antisubmarine warfare than for patrol, she appeared in the late 1950s and followed her predecessors with increased size and performance. Her hull lines benefited from the last of the NACA research and were the final example of that development. Powered by two Wright engines of 1700 horsepower each, she grossed 74,400 pounds and spanned 118 feet. Now the maximum speed had become 240 miles per hour and her normal range was 2000 miles or 3000 miles with a light ferry load.

Martin Marlin P5M-2 boat. The amphibian version was the largest amphibian at 75,000 pounds. (US Coast Guard)

Grumman Albatross UF-1, the last of the Grumman amphibians and still in world-wide use. (US Coast Guard)

Although hardly classified as a patrol plane, the largest of the Grumman twin-engine amphibians should be noted. The Albatross, which first flew in 1948 and continued in production even two months longer than the production life-span of the Catalina, was a most successful general purpose amphibian. Powered by two Wright engines of 1275 horsepower each, she spanned only 80 feet but grossed over 27,000 pounds. With a maximum speed of 265 miles per hour and a range of 2700 miles, she was an excellent flying boat but also thoroughly at home on land. Albatrosses continue in use in wide areas of the world today. If any aircraft could bear the title jack-of-all-trades, the Albatross wins it. The first order, designated HU–16, was from the Navy. The second order was from the Air Force for air–sea rescue operations and designated SA–16. The latter model was a "triphibian," featuring a rugged single ski under the main step permitting successful operations from ice and snow. At least two risky rescue operations of downed and injured crews on the high-altitude plain in central Greenland required the combined use of wheels, hull, and skis to complete each of these missions successfully. With US Navy, Air Force, Marine, Army, and Coast Guard use, plus varied mission operations in a large number of foreign countries, it is probable that this aircraft has the record for ubiquity and utility. It also holds most of the world records in many categories of seaplane performance.

14

THE GIANT FLYING BOATS

Prior to World War II, only a few landplanes had flown across the North Atlantic. By the end of the war thousands of landplanes, even single-engine fighters, had made the crossing. It became an established mode of aviation. Money was unlimited if it hastened victory. Huge concrete airports appeared everywhere on both sides of the ocean. The big airport at Gander, Newfoundland became the takeoff base for all European ferry flights.

Great numbers of Douglas DC–4, four-engined transport and cargo landplanes became available toward the end of the war and went into military service carrying spare parts of high priority to Europe and returning with gravely wounded soldiers. The wartime mission proved the feasibility of peacetime Atlantic passenger flights by landplanes. The significance was not immediately recognized, and the momentum of flying boat development continued through the war and well into the decade of the forties. Many new, efficient transport flying boats continued to appear.

But—they won no orders after the prototypes flew. The day of the giant flying boats had ended. Though they yielded to progress like the great Clipper sailing ships before them, they led the way to a new commerce and should be chronicled.

DORNIER DO–X

The German government and Dornier had their eyes set from the outset on future transatlantic passenger service. As early as 1929 they floated a new world's giant in the form of the twelve-engine DO–X, grossing over 60,000 pounds, by far the largest airplane of her day. She would have been beautiful, except for the six tandem engine nacelles sprouting on struts above the monoplane wing. The aircraft was in advance of the engine development available and was far from a brilliant performer. The hull had the appearance of a junior ocean liner. She captured people's interest all over the world.

In late 1930 she started a flight to New York by way of Lisbon, the Canary Islands, and South America. The flight

Dornier DO-X in New York Harbor—the first of the giants, with the lines of a seagoing vessel. (Smithsonian Institution)

was dogged by many troubles and did not finally arrive in New York until August 1931. Loaded only with fuel for her battery of thirsty engines, she carried no payload. When a wing is flying very close to the water surface it gains lift by squeezing a cushion of air underneath. The long-range flights started by taking off on this cushion. Climbs to a higher altitude could not be made until near the midpoint of each overseas flight. In the course of this journey, she made two open-sea landings when fuel ran short and easily taxied the remainder of the trip to the destination port.

Italy later purchased two DO–Xs, which then successfully flew over the Alps. They were not used in passenger service, as intended, and after takeover by the Italian Navy, quickly vanished into limbo.

SHORT SARAFAND

By far the largest biplane ever flown was the English Short Sarafand in 1935. Weighing 70,000 pounds and spanning 150 feet—extreme for a biplane—she had 5500 horsepower

Short Sarafand with six engines, the world's largest biplane. (Flight International)

from six Rolls–Royce Buzzard water-cooled engines in three tandem nacelles. She flew only 150 mph with a 1450-mile range, and marked the end of England's big biplanes. The gap between the wings was 16 feet, so great that men walking on the lower wing could pass under the bottom of the between-wing nacelles in a standing position.

THE BIG SIKORSKYS

The first large American passenger amphibian, the Sikorsky S–40, appeared in 1931. She followed the proven long-term Sikorsky formula for light structural weight with tail booms, a maze of struts, and with engine nacelles still hanging below the wing. She weighed 34,000 pounds, spanned 114 feet, had 2300 horsepower, and still cruised only 110 mph with a less-than-1000-mile range when carrying twenty-four passengers in the amphibian configuration. As a pure boat with the landing gear removed, she carried forty passengers with better speed and range. At that time such performance was enough to prove the worth of international

Sikorsky S-40 Amphibian, which spread Pan American's wings to South America. (Sikorsky Aircraft)

Sikorsky S-44, the last of the Great Sikorskys. (Sikorsky Aircraft)

Sikorsky S-42 initiated Pan American's Pacific service. (Sikorsky Aircraft)

service. Pan American operated three to South America, flying ten million miles in less than three years.

The somewhat larger and much faster S–42 soon followed in 1934, with four Hornet engines nestled into the leading edge of the wing and the tail at last mounted directly on the longer hull. Even this seaplane still retained a pair of sloping wing struts, but she was fast, with enough range to success-

The first Sikorsky amphibian (top) and the Excaliber (bottom). Quite a change in fifteen years! (Sikorsky Aircraft)

fully pioneer the Pacific runs before the Martins took over the service.

The last of the line of Sikorsky flying boats was the S–44. Three were built just at the start of World War II and named Excaliburs. Their lines were as beautiful as the early Sikorsky's were homely. The first was test flown in January 1942 by Charles F. Blair of Pan American. Though the three had been ordered by American Export Airlines, they were promptly taken over by the US Navy, who used them for an amazing pattern of very long wartime flights to South

America, Africa, and European ports. Captain Blair was at the controls on many flights, including a nonstop against head winds from Ireland to New York. Carrying 4000 gallons of fuel, these great aircraft had nearly 5000 miles range.

One was cracked up in Newfoundland, but the other two flew on into years of peace, even making nonstop flights from Lima to New York. Captain Blair took time off from Pan American to fly five special flights from Lake Minnetonka, Minneapolis, to Iceland. For years the last Excalibur flew the ultrashort run from Long Beach, California to Avalon Island, and undoubtedly has the record for carrying the most passengers of any single seaplane. She was last operated until 1972, again by Captain Blair, for Antilles Airlines in the Virgin Islands.

MARTIN CLIPPERS

In the midthirties, Martin's growing attention to flying boats won the interest of Pan American Airways, who had then decided to conquer the Pacific before the Atlantic. Together they raised specification sights to the farthest border of conceivable attainment. Martin made good with the Model 130, the majestic China Clipper, first flown in 1934. Her long, slim hull, single fin and rudder, gracefully curved bridge pylon above the hull, and beautiful large wing of 130-foot span gave the appearance of serene prowess. Her four engines, the most powerful of the day, fitted snugly into the leading edge of the thick wing. Greatest of all was her 3000-mile range while carrying forty-two passengers at a gross weight of 51,000 pounds. Three were built and established regular Pacific passenger service in the last years before the war with comfort superior to today's passenger accommodations. In 1945 the last of them was still flying regularly to Africa in support of the war effort.

Martin 130, the China Clipper, leaving San Francisco for the Orient. (Pan American Airways)

Martin 156 Soviet Clipper—delivered to Russia and never heard from again! (Martin-Marietta)

Their success inspired Martin to make an even more beautiful successor, the M–156, with a wingspan of 156 feet and gross weight of 63,000 pounds. The first and only one was bought by Soviet Russia just before the war. And after arrival there, it was never heard of again!

BOEING CLIPPERS

Although the first Boeing airplane in 1916 was a float seaplane, Boeing was a latecomer in supplying Pan American with giant flying boats. They caught up decisively in the final days of transocean flying boats. The magnificent Model 314 was powered with four Wright Cyclone engines of 1600 horsepower each. Her span was 150 feet with a gross weight of 60,000 pounds. Twelve were manufactured. Their first Pan American mail crossing of the Atlantic occurred in May 1939. Within a month transatlantic passenger flights were at last a reality, terminating in Lisbon, although special flights later went direct to England. The final international goal of North Atlantic scheduled passenger service was attained after two decades of competition. It continued throughout the war in time to facilitate communication and transportation of Very Important People. Sir Winston Churchill was an enthusiastic passenger who himself enjoyed piloting the great boats whenever aboard.

I made a round trip during the first year of service and have never since crossed the ocean in such sumptuous comfort. The original luxury accommodations were still installed, though stripped out a month later to save weight and provide capacity for more passengers. We boarded via a carpeted vessel's gangplank to the deck of the big sponson and entered the main cabin, as wide as today's "wide-body" jets. An airy corridor extended aft and upward to the series of individual staterooms on each side. By day, seven-foot-long seats faced each other, permitting sociable conversation between the

Boeing 314 Clipper, the queen of the giants who permitted Pan American to finally establish transatlantic service. (Pan American Airways)

four people assigned to each compartment. By night, these seats formed lower berths with upper berths folded down above them. Pullman-type curtains screened off each bunk and individual windows permitted a look outside. In today's wide-body jets only two out of ten passengers have the privilege of a window. Full-course dinners with wine were served in the main saloon on broad, damask-covered tables like those in the Martin Clippers before them. As on luxury liners, there were two "seatings," announced by a liveried waiter ringing a ship's dinner bell. And—honest, I'm not exaggerating—the English gentlemen aboard came down to the saloon in dinner jackets!

On the return flight it was Captain Marius Lodeesen's first crossing as full captain in charge. He invited me up to the bridge. I marveled at the spaciousness of the pilothouse with its large flight deck behind the pilot's seats. Here was the navigator's table with sextant sighting hatch above and the engineer's post with four banks of engine-monitoring instru-

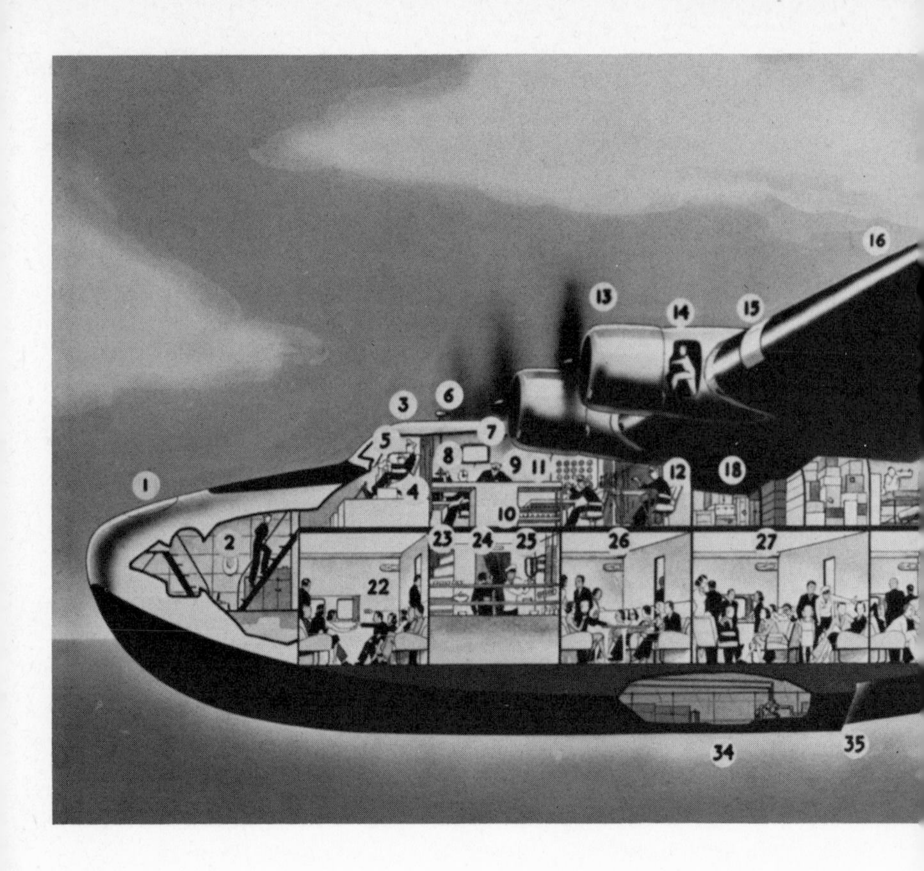

ments and controls. I asked the purpose of two padded sound-deadening doors on each side of this area. The navigator opened one, and with a surge of engine noise, we looked into the corridor nearly four feet in diameter, extending out to the engine nacelles through the leading edge of the wing.

I asked Captain Lodeesen if I might crawl out. With a smile he said he'd come also. Passing the inboard engine, we continued to the outboard nacelle and sat there facing each other. The deafening roar of the great Cyclone engine prevented any conversation, but by gesturing, he indicated a removable panel in the fire wall. Pretending to use an in-

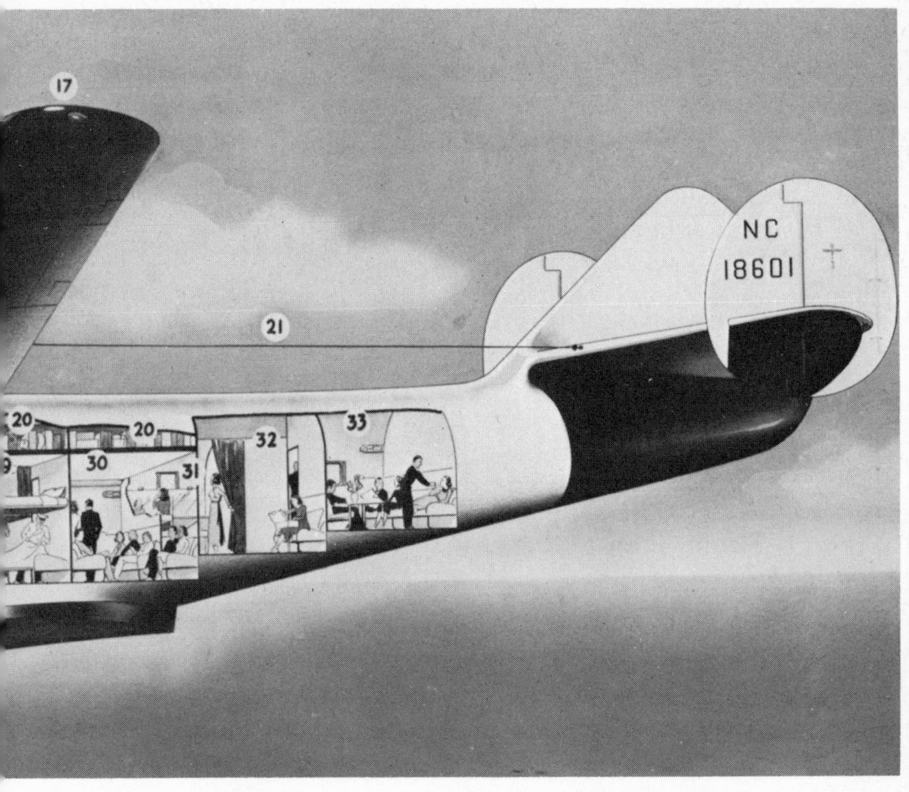

Boeing 314 accommodations. Note mechanic in engine nacelle at 14. (Pan American Airways)

visible screwdriver, and by rapidly tapping his forefinger on his thumb to indicate the sparking of a magneto, he demonstrated that engine accessory repairs could be made in flight. An apparent access door in the side of the monocoque nacelle turned out to be a spring-loaded outside footstep. The Captain reached over and sprung it open so we could peer out.

GOOD GRIEF!

Right alongside, in the middle of the ocean, another Boeing Clipper was flying tight formation with us! *Incredible!* It was too close! Then I realized that the hull, a full 60 feet away, was our own ship. Back in the quiet of the flight deck I sheepishly joined the laughter of the crew. It was a trick often played on visitors. Lodeesen himself had experienced the same illusion.

Pan American ordered twelve of these great aircraft. When the United States entered the war, three were diverted to British Overseas Airways and the Navy commandeered the fleet, using only one and permitting Pan Am to continue with the other eight, three of which were in Pacific service. Pan Am's last flight terminated in San Francisco in April 1946. No passenger was ever lost at sea, even though Pan Am landed once in the open Pacific because of multiple engine failure, and a charter operator later ran out of fuel over the Atlantic. Both landings were free of any damage, and all passengers were taken off. Both planes were sunk as derelicts by gunfire. The remaining Boeings had a checkered career in charter service with long periods of inactivity at their moorings. The last was finally scrapped in 1951.

OTHER GIANTS

Short Brothers in England seemed to pull ahead of their rivals with the Empire class of boat in 1936, and after the war they flew one more huge passenger boat, the Shetland. The French Company of Latecoere strove to capture the Atlantic prize with a double-decked, six-engine monoplane of 70,000 pounds in 1935. Later, the Sud–Est Model 200 with six engines totaling 9000 horsepower at 72,000 pounds gross was under construction when the Germans invaded France. They supervised the continued construction of three for their own purposes. All were destroyed on the ground or water in later fighting.

Finally, after the war, Latecoere flew a beautiful long-hulled, six-engine boat of 86,000 pounds with more than

1947 Latecoere 631 with typically beautiful French lines—but she flew too late. (Smithsonian Institution)

Martin JRM-1 Mars. Four of these cargo planes shuttled to Hawaii during W.W. II. (US Navy)

transatlantic range, cruising at 190 mph. Her retractable tip floats folded into the outboard nacelles. She might have won international honors—if she hadn't been too late. Germany, too, made a last stab at the expiring business with a Blohm and Vass Model 238, designed as a patrol plane during the war. She was a real giant, spanning 197 feet, grossing 148,000 pounds, with a range well over 3000 miles.

MARTIN MARS

The largest American flying boat ever to see service was the Mars JRM–1. Powered with four Wright engines providing 8000 horsepower, three were delivered to the Navy during the war as cargo carriers shuttling between San Francisco and Hawaii on a fast schedule. Two more, then grossing as high as 165,000 pounds, were delivered after the war. They spanned 200 feet and cruised at an economical 155 mph, though their top speed was 220 mph. On a proving flight, one flew 4600 miles nonstop in thirty-two hours. The other once carried three hundred passengers from San Francisco to San Diego. Two of the Mars planes, based on a lake in Vancouver Island, are still flying as the world's largest water bombers.

HUGHES HERCULES

The largest, the queerest, the most controversial of them all was the mammoth Hughes Hercules—460,000 pounds, spanning 310 feet, powered by eight Pratt and Whitney engines for a total of 24,000 horsepower. In 1947 she flew only once, in a straight line a little longer and a little higher than the Wright Brothers' Kitty Hawk flight forty-four years previously.

However queer her background, she was not queer in

Hughes Hercules, the largest of the giants. (Smithsonian Institution)

appearance. She was a beautiful seaplane, pure of line, uncluttered. Howard Hughes always contended that he alone was the sole designer. Born of a truly patriotic attempt by Hughes and Henry J. Kaiser, a government order for three was placed in 1942. Envisioned for wartime transport, she was designed to carry key supplies and soldiers over the Atlantic's submarine-infested waters and across the huge Pacific, avoiding the intolerable delay of shipments by slow vessels. But in wartime no further priorities on aluminum could be issued; so she was constructed entirely of wood! Birch was the common material of the structure, along with poplar, maple, balsa, and some spruce. No doubt she was well overweight compared to equivalent aluminum structures. Although three times heavier than the Martin Mars, the payload for a 2500-mile flight was 58,000 pounds, only 17,000 pounds more. The estimated cost in production would have been five times more. Still in existence in her huge, secret, well-guarded, humidified hangar, she goes down in

Hughes Hercules hull interior. No wonder she was called "The Spruce Goose." (Smithsonian Institution)

history under the name of the "Spruce Goose" or the "Flying Lumber Yard."

SAUNDERS–ROE PRINCESS

As late as 1953, England could not turn away from her beloved big seagoing ships of the air. Under government order, Saunders–Roe constructed three magnificent SR–45 Princess flying boats. Each grossed 315,000 pounds, spanned 310 feet, and was powered with all the thrust she could get, though still below the optimum for such a gigantic craft. Each used ten Bristol Proteus engines. Four pairs were coupled to counterrotating propellers. Outboard of them on each side was another Proteus driving a single prop to complete the full complement of ten. Their top speed was 380 mph, with fuel available for a 5500-mile range.

The big innovation was pressurization of the two passenger decks. To accomplish this without an absurdly narrow hull diameter, there were three circular sections the length of the hull, one above the other, the decks of which tied the curved lobed sides together to hold the pressure. Below the lower lobe, or "hold," the conventional bottom flared out to a beam as wide as the circular sections above, providing a very strong but light bottom structure. All three were assembled, but only the first one flew—and flew well, appearing in flight for several years at the Farnborough Air Show and other public functions.

Very little attention was given to their ultimate scrapping.

Saunders Roe Princess with ten engines, the last of the giants in 1953. (Smithsonian Institution)

15

RECENT DEVELOPMENTS

TURBINES

The initial "static thrust" of propellers is greatest at zero speed and decreases as taxiing and air speed increase. Conversely, the thrust of jet engines is least at zero speed but increases steadily with flight speed and altitude. Because water resistance during water takeoff is much greater than rolling resistance during land takeoffs, it is not surprising that turbine-powered seaplanes have lagged far behind equivalent landplanes. Saunders–Roe made a few small twin-engine fighter seaplanes. They performed well and doubtless were the fastest of all seaplanes, about equal to equivalent land jet fighters. The air intake was in the very bow, with only moderate freeboard. One wonders what would happen if that intake were submerged in rough water.

The most ambitious jet seaplane was Martin's P6M Seamaster, powered by four Pratt and Whitney J–75 jets, grossing 160,000 pounds with 100-foot span. She flew in 1959 and featured sharply swept-back wings with negative dihedral, which brought the tips so close to the water the floats had no struts. Her combat radius was only 1500 miles, but air refueling would have been used as on land jet bombers of

Saunders Roe Twin Jet Fighter. (Flight International)

Martin P6M Seamaster with four jet engines. (US Navy)

the time. Seamaster was a terrific airplane with flight performance practically equal to the equivalent Boeing land-based bombers. Her top speed was more than 0.8 Mach. Seven were built, but as it did with so many other postwar prototypes, the Navy soon canceled the orders, probably because the envisioned mission did not materialize.

A few years later, Soviet Russia flew a fast flying boat that looked very much like the Seamaster. She was powered with two jets of 15,000 pounds thrust each. A photograph was about the only information published in the US.

The last of the Convair flying boats was also turbine-powered—the P5Y, named the Tradewind. She was powered with four Allison T–40 turboprops, driving counterrotating propellers, and grossing 45,000 pounds. Her cruising speed was 285 mph with a very short range because her mission was beach assault, landing troops, tanks, and other heavy equipment, possibly under fire. For this purpose, there was a large bow entrance hatch raised to unload over a ramp onto the sand. A few were built and saw about three years' service.

Convair P5Y Tradewind with counter rotating props driven by Allison Turbines. (US Navy)

Japanese Shin-Meiwa PS-1 with five turbines—one producing powered lift. (Shin-Meiwa Aircraft)

While Convair was sponsoring delta-winged fighters, they still hoped to benefit from their reputation for excellent seaplanes. It was natural for them to try a waterborne jet fighter. The Sea Dart was a most courageous design featuring water skis. (She is described in detail and illustrated in Chapter 19, page 237.)

Japan, a nation of islands, still retains a great interest in big flying boats. The Shin–Meiwa 94,000-pound boat is a very progressive five-engined design for patrol and anti-submarine missions. She is more capable of operating in and out of rougher water than any previous seaplane. In addition to being very compact and ruggedly built, she is a true STOL (capable of Short Takeoff Or Landing). The four main engines are General Electric T–64 turboprops of 3400 horsepower each. The fifth engine in the center section is a GE T–58 of 1400 horsepower used to "blow" the wings; that is, to provide a sheath of blown air over the large slotted flaps, greatly increasing the lift and reducing the landing speed. It is so effective in diverting lifting air downwards that spray actually blows forward under the wing just before touching the wave tops.

Extinguishing forest fires became a new mission for seaplanes in the late 1950s. Canadair Limited of Montreal developed a modern amphibian for the purpose and won

Canadair CL-214 Water Bomber in French Service; she is in current production as a fire fighter. (Canadair Ltd.)

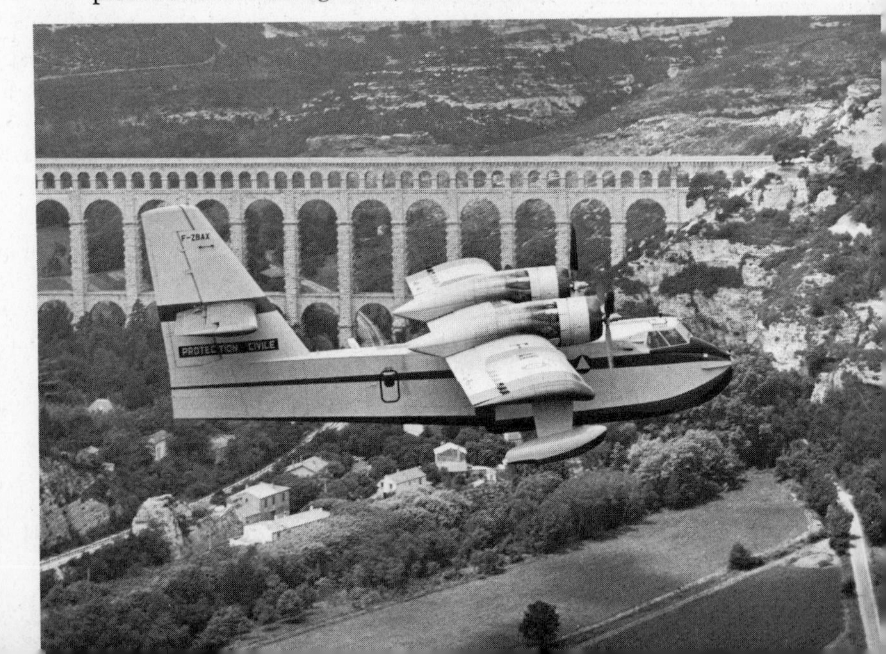

Canadair CL-214 extinguishing a forest fire in a mountain pass. (Canadair Ltd.)

orders in many countries. Their CL–215 monoplane is powered by two Pratt and Whitney 2100-horsepower propeller engines, grosses 34,000 pounds and spans 94 feet. A main compartment in the hull is a huge water tank with a retractable scoop in front and a dumping ramp behind. She lands in the nearest lake to the fire, scoops up a full load of water, and is back to drop it on the blaze, all in a few minutes. The ships are most effective in wilderness areas, though a small fleet is operating in France.

SMALL UTILITY AND PERSONAL SEAPLANES

So the huge flying boats have faded into history. We are left with the wonderful, plentiful, useful small flying boats and floatplanes steadily increasing in numbers. How did we get here? What can be said about their history? There are too many items to possibly record. The British Navy long adhered to utility single-engine flying amphibians, the Seagulls, first pusher, then tractor, and later the single-engine Sea Lions. There were Saunders–Roe singles and twins. Dornier had many small designs, Rohrbach too, and Heinkel had a fine small amphibian, but there were no frontiers in Europe and few private owners. None of them flourished, including a continuous flow of lovely little French designs. A few were made in this country under license, including the Schreck, known as the Viking here, a few of which saw long Coast Guard service watching the fishing fleet and giving hurricane warnings. Another was the small Italian Savoia–Marchetti three-place amphibian.

In this country the Curtiss Seagull yielded to the Ireland Neptune and Loening Commuter. Fokker made one excellent seven-passenger amphibian. Then came the brilliant Fleet Wings Sea Bird, designed by James C. Reddig. Made

The incomparable Fleet Wings Sea Bird owned by Channing Clark.

Viking OO-1. Note flat bottom. Author was Chief Engineer. (US Coast Guard)

American-built Savoia-Marchetti S56. (American Aeronautical Corp.)

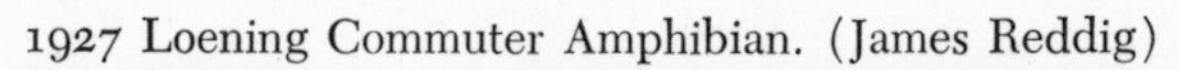
1927 Loening Commuter Amphibian. (James Reddig)

American Fokker with ingenious hinged seawing landing gear. Mr. Anthony Fokker is stepping out of the cabin. (James Reddig)

of stainless steel, she was a pure delight to fly, but the Great Depression squelched any real production.

There were many others. A couple of years after the war, Grumman Widgeons went out of production—prematurely. The existing ships were converted to more modern flat-six engines with more power and better performance. Many were sold out of this country, and if you can find one today, you'll pay nearly three times their original price of thirty years ago. Goose and Widgeon manufacture yielded to the beautiful Grumman Mallard, with two 600-horsepower Pratt and Whitneys and capacity for eight or ten people. One purchaser who had owned a Goose and a Widgeon before bought two, using one and retaining the other as an investment. Sure enough, the demand increased enough in a year for him to sell the second at the new list price gaining a handsome profit. The military needs of the Korean War ended Mallard production—again prematurely.

The Thurston Skimmer amphibian, designed by David Thurston, appeared in 1955. Thurston sold forty-four and then sold the design to the Lake Aircraft Company. To date, a total of almost four hundred have been delivered. Dave more recently designed the excellent, very simple, two-passenger Teal amphibian now being manufactured by the Schweizer Company of Elmira, New York.

The Republic Aircraft Company of Farmingdale, Long Island, plunged from wartime fighter aircraft to making four-place Sea Bee amphibians. Though slow and very noisy, they became instantly popular. Over a thousand were delivered at a sales price unfortunately below the manufacturing cost.

Lake Buccanere on a ramp. (Lake Aircraft)

Schweizer-Thurston Teal Amphibian. Though only a two-passenger, she has won surprising export demand. (Schweizer Aircraft)

About this time a neat four-passenger, twin-engine amphibian began appearing around the Mediterranean, made by the Piaggio Company of Genoa. The Kearny–Trecker Company of Milwaukee secured a license to assemble and sell them in this country under the name of the Royal Gull, and a few are still flying.

SPORT AVIATION ASSOCIATION

Recently, under the sponsorship of the Experimental Aircraft Association, an increasing number of home-designed and home-built airplanes of one-, two-, and four-passenger capacity have flown. There are now about three thousand of these sport airplanes. The fun of personal flying has turned many of these amateur, but very skillful, designers and builders to small flying boats and amphibians.

A typical but outstanding member of the EAA is Percival H. Spencer, originally from Connecticut. In 1914, at the age of seventeen, Spence soloed in his own successful flying boat. The following year he designed and built a larger two-place flying boat and made passenger hops from the Connecticut River. In 1919, Spence designed and built a three-place, single-float seaplane in Boston. He used it to carry passengers over Cape Cod from his base at Onset, Massachusetts. This led to his becoming the first sales, training, and charter operator at the Hartford Municipal Airport.

After the profitable sale of his business, Spence again turned to his pet interest in small flying boats. For several years he carried a model of an ultrasimple concept in his car. He then proposed purchasing a single Edo float and making a streamlined cabin on the deck for two passengers in tandem. With a monoplane wing above the passengers, and with a pusher engine operating between outrigger tail booms, he had a basic and simple concept. In the 1930s, he gave his expertise to the Spencer–Larson Company, which made a rather advanced small amphibian, but with strong Larson input. This little plane featured an engine in the hull driving through a vertical shaft to an overhead pusher propeller. It is doubtful if this engine location was wholly acceptable to Spence. The aircraft flew well, but the war came. We next knew Spence when he had sold his original design concept to Republic Aviation. It became their Sea Bee, but with the tail now mounted on the hull.

Spence then retired to Florida on a houseboat, but soon in California he turned back again to a design now called the Spencer Amphibian Air Car. A four-place pusher again, it is an advancement along the same general lines as the Sea Bee. In 1970, Spence took off in his amphib to attend the annual EAA Convention in Oshkosh. Again, in 1971, he attended Oshkosh and continued on to Hartford with a delightful zigzag sightseeing return flight to California. All this at the age of seventy-five.

Now he has a thriving business selling plans and parts for

home builders to make their own aircraft to his design. It features the use of steel tubing, wood, and fiberglass, each in the places where it is most adaptable to simple construction using handtools. The parts he sells are only the specialty items requiring tooling and skill usually in excess of home builders' equipment. (See figure 16, pp. 250-251).

EDO

Meanwhile, back at the float farm in College Point, Long Island, the Edo Aircraft Corporation, now called the Edo Commercial Corporation, steadily increased the sale of twin-floats for installation under nearly every utility landplane. Before the war, they pioneered a pair of amphibian floats with main wheels forward and tail wheels at the sterns. The center of gravity was naturally high, and it was a bit cranky to handle on land. Since the war, they have made amphibian floats with the main wheels retracting just behind the step with retractable nose wheels in the bows. These handle well, even on moderately rough fields, though they make a pretty lofty airplane on the ground, particularly in smaller sizes.

Conversions of Cessna landplanes and their rivals are growing in popularity. Canadians install amphibious floats on DeHaviland Beavers, Otters, and turboprop Twin Otters. Now, several other amphibious float manufacturers are getting into the act, notably Pee Kay DeVore, Inc. of Roslyn Heights, New York, Wipline, Inc. of Inver Grove Heights, Minnesota, and Aqua Float Corp. of Lino Lakes, Minnesota.

The extent of water flying is often overlooked because a thousand seaplanes at individual bases are much less obvious to the general public than a thousand equivalent landplanes based on airports. Recent advances in seaplane design and operation are just as great as for landplanes even though seaplanes are fewer in number. A bright future lies ahead for more water flying.

16

GENERAL DESIGN PROBLEMS

Seaplane pilots and engineers both seek the same objective: safe, efficient, and economical flight from water. The engineer's job comes first and is much more difficult than the design of landplanes. It is a blend of hydrodynamics and aerodynamics, often called aeroGodamnics by those who labor to mate them! The seaplane designer needs a "feel" for his designs beyond the mere knowledge of engineering principles. He must know almost intuitively where water "wants" to go, and when it must be prevented from going there. He directs water to produce the maximum lift for takeoff and suppresses as much as possible the inevitable spray. The more water flying he has personally enjoyed, the better he is as a designer.

CONFIGURATIONS

"Configuration" is the term used to define the general arrangement of an aircraft. It defines the location and relation of all the basic components required to make a successful airplane type. Past and present seaplane configurations far exceed those of landplanes both in number and variety.

All airplanes require wings, a fuselage, a tail, a landing gear, and a power plant. The plant includes the propeller or fan or jet, or even a helicopter rotor. For a seaplane, the equivalent "landing gear" is more complex, requiring flotation and stability on the water and hydrodynamic lift during takeoff and landing. Provisions for handling the seaplane on the water are a further necessary complication. It must taxi well under good control, be easy to board and debark, and have special means for easy docking and mooring. Amphibians, in addition, require wheeled landing gears that must be retracted, a consideration that cannot be an afterthought.

In a sense, seaplane configurations parallel the many varied rigs of sailing vessels, leading to just as heated discussions among pilots as among yachtsmen regarding their relative merits—providing fun around the fireside on winter nights. An understanding of past and present configurations is a necessary prelude to a discussion of detailed design problems.

THREE-FLOAT CONFIGURATIONS

In the early days, it was logical to convert landplanes into floatplanes by replacing each of the three wheels with a float at the same location. It will be remembered that Fabre's first successful seaplane had the equivalent of a tricycle gear. There was a single float under the bow and a pair of floats under the stern. In England, after the configuration of the classic tractor landplane was established, a pair of floats was placed where wheels had been, with a tail float in place of the tail skid. Neither of these configurations is seen today.

Another early seaplane configuration was the tailless Burgess–Dunne seaplane. Many tailless airplanes have flown.

They secure longitudinal control by radical wing sweep-back, which places the elevators on the wing tip, usually deflecting differentially for roll control. The Burgess–Dunne had a short main float under the fuselage and a pair of floats under each wing tip. Perhaps this would have been called a single float, except that all three had to bear in the water when the plane was at rest to provide flotation stability.

TWIN-FLOAT CONFIGURATIONS

No one refers to twin-float seaplanes as catamarans, but they are, and have become the most popular in civil use. N–struts usually support each float, with cross struts and wires between. Occasionally, they are mounted on streamlined cantilevered pedestals. Several good seaplanes have reduced the drag of struts and wires by mounting the floats at the knuckles of inverted gull wings. That is, the wing slopes down from the fuselage to the point of attachment and then resumes a steep rising dihedral angle to the wing tip. A few catamaran seaplanes have elongated the floats into tail booms back to the stabilizer.

Cessna Skywagon showing all details of Edo Amphibious floats. (Edo Aircraft)

SINGLE-FLOAT CONFIGURATIONS

The early Curtiss seaplanes used a single float stabilized delicately by rudimentary wing-tip floats. This single-float method was popular for several decades with the United States Navy. Many training planes and shipboard scouts featured a large single float under a basic landplane with small floats under the wing tips. It was believed to be a lighter configuration than a twin-float with less water skin friction and was thought to be faster in the air for the same reason. The propeller was better protected from spray. Ruggedness in severe rough water was a further advantage, compared with racking stresses in twin-float strutting systems. You can guess they were very difficult to board. The pilot had to climb around the sides of the fuselage above him before reaching the cockpit, and there was no deck space available for anchoring or docking. This configuration is now considered obsolete.

Early Navy Vought Corsair on single Grumman Amphibious float. (Edward Jablonski)

HELICOPTER FLOATS

Since helicopters can land literally anywhere, except in trees or on the side of a hill, there is almost no reason why they should operate from the water. However, as a precaution, copters often have pneumatic floats to permit safe water landings when necessary. Inflatable floats are extremely light, and slow-speed taxiing does not require a precise hull bottom shape. They also make good gears for land landings, now that improved rotor design has nearly eliminated the old ground resonance problem. Ground handling becomes a problem because the ship cannot be moved easily with the rotor stopped. Other very neat pneumatic emergency floats are available attached to the top of the landing skids. They are "reefed," or folded tightly to the skid, until required. Then compressed-air bottles are tripped, fully inflating the floats almost instantly. When rotors are spinning on the water, they provide lateral stability and control even when the floats are narrowly spaced. However, when the rotors are stopped, stability on the water is meager.

FLYING BOATS

There are a few half-breeds, but basically "floats" carry none of the useful load, and "hulls" carry it all, including passengers and cargo. Essentially, wings and tails are attached to the hull. Engines are mounted above or on the wing. Shorter hulls with tails mounted on outriggers have nearly disappeared. Flying boats are stabilized on the water by small floats under the wing tips or by larger floats near the hull. As an alternate, many boats in the past, particularly the larger ones, used sponsons for "sea wings." Airfoil-shaped stubs projected from the hull near the center of gravity at the waterline. Reduced air drag was the basic advantage.

The previously mentioned Italian long-range Savoia–Marchetti flying boats were true catamarans. The large identical twin hulls were short, with outriggers to the tail. The pilots sat side by side on the center line, almost buried in the leading edge of the thick wing. Though obviously unsuited for passenger service in double cabins, these offered few disadvantages for military operations. They might have been erratic performers in very heavy seas.

Several prototype "triphibians" have flown in the past, so called because they offered the owner either a landplane, a seaplane, or an amphibian simply by detaching either the hull or the landing gear. The deck of the hull bolted to the flat bottom of the fuselage with blending lines. A pretty tall landing gear retracted into either the wings or the fuselage. Of course, wing-tip floats were also detachable. The scheme provides an easily convertible airplane but it usually ends up heavier and more costly than a pure amphibian. If it is single engine, the prop must be so high it spoils forward visibility, or an overhead nacelle is required, which impairs the landplane vision.

Sikorsky HH-3F. US Coast Guard Amphibian Air Sea Rescue Helicopter. (US Coast Guard)

The Blackburn Company of England once flew a retractable-hull seaplane. Designed for a military mission requiring speed and range, she was twin-engine with a nearly conventional fuselage. The hull, or single float, whichever it was called, swung upward when airborne and retracted tight against the fuselage.

There are a few helicopter flying boats used for Air Sea Rescue missions. They can taxi directly to a raft or use a rescue hoist.

SPRAY CONSIDERATIONS

The renowned Anthony H.G. Fokker, known as "Tony" to all in aviation, once remarked that all airplanes would look different "if we could see the air spray." He once flabbergasted a young US Coast Guard flight crew by attempting to do just that. When the first Fokker "Antares" twin-engine flying boat was delivered to the Coast Guard, they complained that the ailerons "nibbled" at high speed. Characteristically, Fokker went himself to investigate the complaint. He took off and, after confirming the shudder, left the pilot's seat and went to the hatch in the cabin roof set in the upper surface of the smooth cantilever wing. The two pilots knew he stood up in the hatch, but didn't know he had actually crawled out onto the wing surface until the ship became a little left-wing heavy.

To their horror, they saw one of his arms crooked over the leading edge of the wing, and stared helplessly as he slowly inched his way farther out. When he was as far out as the inboard edge of the aileron, he explored the airflow by spoiling it with his free arm. He found he could either induce or relieve the shudder. Returning carefully, he dropped back into the cabin, sure that he had found the cause. He had "seen" the spray.

There is no trouble in seeing the spray when a seaplane is operating on the water! Unlike the simple layout of a landplane, the whole configuration is dedicated to suppressing as much spray as possible. A flying boat becomes more efficient as the spray is reduced.

First of all, a flying boat *is* a boat—but with wings. The hull must satisfy the requirements of every boat. The center of buoyancy must be under the center of gravity, and the displacement must be adequate for the weight. It must have enough freeboard to prevent swamping in waves. To be moderately seaworthy at slow speed, the bow must be relatively high. Already we are forced to depart from the classic fuselage lines even before considering propeller location. There is one relief; since the flying boat is stabilized laterally on the water by auxiliary floats, we need not design the hull cross sections to prevent capsize, and the center of gravity may be far above the center of buoyancy. As soon as the speed exceeds that of a displacement boat, the hull must plane. Spray starts flying and must be suppressed by skillful design of the bottom lines.

17

BOTTOM DESIGN

Both the laternal and longitudinal lines of a hull are shaped to push the water downwards and achieve a maximum lifting force. The forebody of a flying boat, the part ahead of the step, is almost identical with the bottom of a speedboat or planing outboard. Unlike the speedboat, however, the flying boat must rotate or pitch up to gain the most wing lift either for takeoff or landing. The speedboat should run at a constant trim angle, and the center of gravity may be far ahead of the transom, the sharp edge at the stern where the water leaves the hull. The transom becomes the step of a seaplane hull. It has to be placed nearly as far forward as the center of gravity to permit rotation about it.

The afterbody refers to the part of the hull astern of the step. The aircraft could take off and land perfectly on smooth water if there were no afterbody, but it is needed for flotation in the displacement attitude. Then it too must plane during parts of the run. In outrigger configurations, the afterbody length is determined mainly by static displacement requirements, though the hull must be as long as a fuselage when it supports the flying tail.

Bottom loading, the number of pounds per square foot of bottom area, is not unlike wing loading. A lot of planing area is needed for lift at low speed but gives excessive drag as the speed increases. Merely a few feet of bottom, just ahead of the step, provides a lot of lift at high water speeds with little drag. All these considerations resulted in a myriad of ideas and designs that have finally stabilized in recent years with only moderate variations.

Designers make frequent reference to center lines, but they are more difficult to establish on a flying boat than on a landplane. Usually, landplane thrust lines, floor lines, and window lines are parallel to a center line, established by the designer at the start of his first profile drawing. Before swept-back vertical tail surfaces became the style, the rudder post was perpendicular to the center line. On landplanes the center line of the wing chord is usually parallel to the center line. As shown in figure 2 (p. 37), all design angles are fundamental and related to the illusive center line. It is a poor three-view drawing that does not clearly show the designer's choice of center line. When it is not shown, floor lines or window lines now seem to be the best clue.

LATERAL SHAPE

Figure 11 shows the classic bottom cross-sectional shapes used over the years. Internal dotted lines indicate the major hull frame members. The pure *flat bottom* (A) is the most obvious and simplest. Since it provides the most planing lift for the least surface, it was naturally used first on the early seaplanes. This type was still in use during the twenties by the French Schreck designs and their licensee in this country, the Viking Flying Boat Company. As chief engineer and test pilot, I found that flat bottoms spank woefully in waves and are heavy because the resulting bottom stresses are very

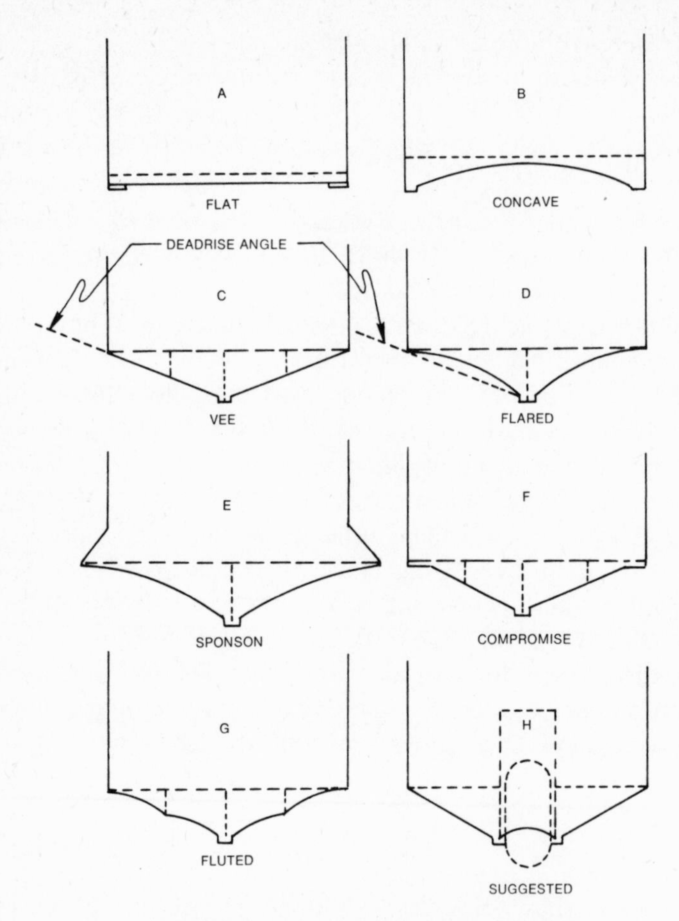

Figure 11—Lateral Bottom Shapes

high. To reduce wave impacts at the step, Schreck designs used a pronounced "tadpole" shape in the sides of the hull. Widest at the pilot's seat forward, it narrowed very rapidly so that the beam at the step was only two-thirds the forward beam, after which the sides were slightly concave back to the tail post. Spray characteristics were excellent in calm water but soon lost the advantage in waves. Vikings taxied on their bottoms up and down wet wooden ramps with ease.

Concave bottoms (B), popular with the Savoia–Marchetti Company, provide a maximum of lift for a given beam. I never flew one, but it seems reasonable to assume that spray out at the side during the period of climbing onto the step should have been well suppressed. It probably "squirted" forward under the bow (even though it changed there to a slight V section), until a fast enough plane was established for foaming water to depart at the step. Keels of vessels are heavy members and take the major bottom loads. Loads on flying boat bottoms are transmitted by the frames to the sides, which become the major strength members. The arched tunnel bottom should lead to light frames, and the bottom skin would be happily in tension.

Nowadays, every powerboat intended to cruise over twelve knots has a *V bottom* (C) with "hard chines" forming a sharp angle with the bottom. Chines are the longitudinal members at the juncture of the bottom and sides. Even in round-bottom boats there is usually a strong fore-and-aft member at about this point even if it cannot be seen as a break in the curved side. The term "hard chines" implies that they provide a water break so that water flowing outwards from under the hull leaves it clean, in a feather of spray. Thus, maximum lift is obtained and there is no additional drag-producing wetted area up the sides.

Obviously, the first entry on landing will be softer than a flat bottom. The "dead rise angle" has varied greatly. Rohrbach, a German designer, used a very deep V on very narrow hulls, resulting in good deep-sea characteristics, though his technique was not adopted by other companies. The favored dead-rise angle seems to have settled between 20 and 25 degrees. Spray flies off at this angle. Sheets of bottom skin, either metal or plywood, are delightfully flat and simple to build.

The *flared bottom* (D) provides better hydrodynamics. "Worked" or double-curved bottom skins are required, as well as frame members, leading to more difficult and expensive manufacture. Spray is turned flat outwards before leaving the hull, thus capturing more lift than a straight V. The dead-rise angle is now measured on a tangent from the keel to the chine. Most of the wave load occurs at the chine, and the skin is under tension. The cross frames become lighter. In general, it has softer characteristics than a simple V.

In the World War I days of flying boats, low power dictated large wing area and lift-off at slow speed. Getting through the hump required a maximum of bottom area, and *sponsons* (E) came into vogue, but were soon abandoned.

A *compromise section* (F) is popular. All the flare occurs at the chine, permitting flat bottom sheets, except for a narrow strip with double curvature at the edges.

Edo floats have long used *fluted bottoms* (G). An intermediate hard chine is inserted a short distance aft of the bow and runs back to the step. These bottoms give maximum lift and are soft in a seaway. Spray characteristics are excellent. Skin drag is reduced toward the end of the takeoff run when the ship planes on only the inside flares, the outside flared section running completely dry—at least in smooth water. Edo owners have considered these fluted bottoms well worth the moderate expense.

Bottom H has no name and, as far as we know, has never been used. It is suggested particularly for amphibians with wheels extending through the bottom. It should have hydrodynamic and structural advantages and provide convenient strength members for the retractable landing gear. Some metal floats are now subordinating cross frames by filling the "cheeks" with styrofoam or other foamed plastics. The longitudinal compartmentalization between the double keels might assist this technique by providing a strong metal box section to take nose wheel loads while increasing spacing between frames.

SPRAY STRIPS

Just as the boat is climbing onto the step, spray leaves the chines far forward regardless of the type of bottom cross section. Wind blows it onto the windshield and into the prop. Many commercial operators attach spray strips after becoming tired of dressing the prop leading edges. They take a variety of shapes, as shown in figure 12. Usually, the external chine member is a bent angle with a very short outward projection pointing downwards about 30 degrees (I). This provides an attachment point for a strip as shown in (J). Because strips add air drag and are subject to bending when they rub on a dock, they are attached only a short way fore and aft, say for the second quarter of the whole forebody. In calm water it is easy to see that the spray blister is poured back into the water surface, where it creates its own upward-thrown spray that can enter the prop discs of twin-engine boats. However, this is only a momentary detriment. In rough water, the extended spray strips may cause more spray; it is a debatable improvement. *Dams* (K) have been used on a very few flying boats. They can be said to capture the spray instead of deflecting it, and provide a noticeable lifting of the bow at hump speed. Since the sides of the hull are curving inward toward the bow at the point where they are attached, considerable air drag is created.

Both strips and dams, particularly the latter, give appreciable aerodynamic lift at the bow just before landing at high-pitch angles, enough to reduce the amount of stabilizer adjustment needed for neutral trim.

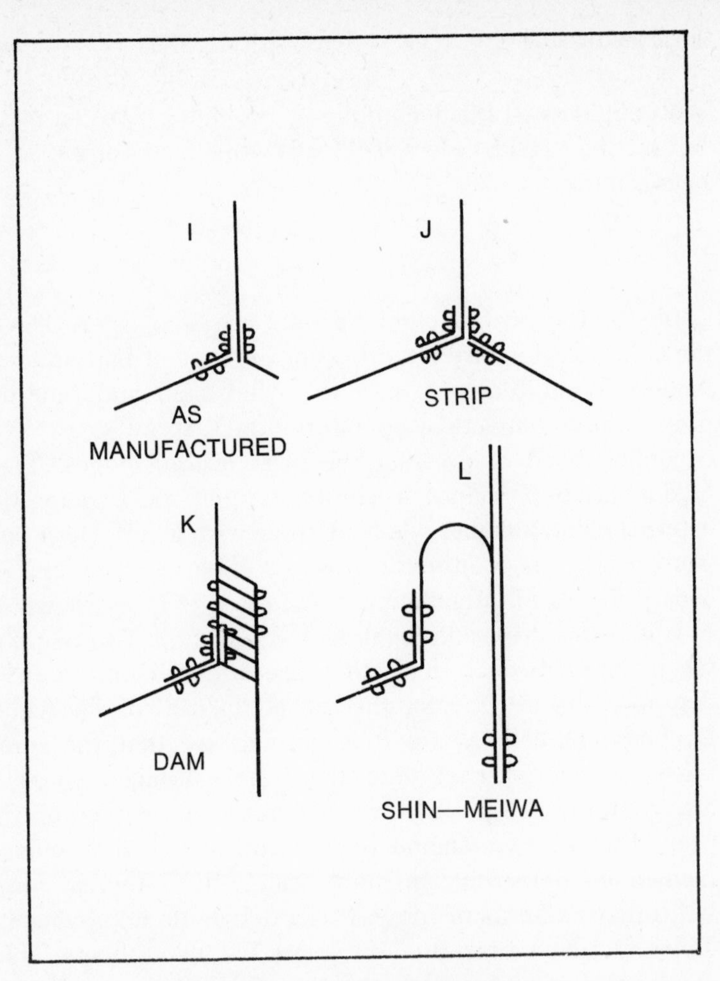

Figure 12—Spray Strips

The large Japanese Shin–Meiwa five-engine flying boat has unique *spray-channels* (L). Designed to operate in the heaviest of seas, and with the fifth engine providing powered lift over the flaps, this device becomes most effective. It swallows the spray off the forebody at the chines and ducts it aft to discharge at the step. Motion pictures in an enormous sea show the success of this modification.

LONGITUDINAL SHAPE

The resistance of a hull moving through water is the sum of the skin friction and the wave-making drag. The latter is unimportant at planing speed, as shown by the wake, which then contains only small waves. Since skin drag increases with speed, the designer makes every effort to keep as much of the hull as possible out of the water while planing.

STEPS

Steps are necessary, but they are a nuisance. The sharp break in the bottom introduces stress concentrations. Worse, it produces a lot of air drag behind. Air flowing beyond the sharp edge breaks into worse turbulence than it would if it flowed toward a sharp vertical edge such as a vertical windshield. The turbulence makes a steady pounding racket on the bottom plates. Igor Sikorsky filed many patents on concepts to streamline the step during flight, though they were never applied.

Steps reduce skin friction while planing by allowing the water to flow free of the hull behind—up to a point. Main steps are located just slightly behind the center of gravity. Common practice is to put the step at an angle from 16 to 24 degrees to a vertical through the normal center of gravity, which is also about the range for main wheel location on tricycle landing gears. When the step is farther aft, heavy elevator pull is required to rotate the craft into a takeoff angle. In the early twenties, double steps were popular. The first step was at the center of gravity or even a little ahead. The second step followed about one beam length farther aft. The after keel line raised a few degrees behind the front step and a few more degrees behind the after step, permitting an easy increase in pitch angle with slight change in control force. Double steps also ameliorated pronounced pitch changes at first touchdown in large waves. Either they disappeared about 1930 or it could be said the second step moved aft when more attention was paid to afterbody lines. But first, let us consider forebody lines.

FOREBODY LINES

The angle of the forebody keel is usually parallel to the center line, though it occasionally slopes downward toward the bow a few degrees. As discussed in Part One, it is related to the angle of incidence attaching the wing to the hull. In profile, common practice runs keel lines and chine lines straight from the step forward to about the two-thirds point of the forebody length measured forward from the step. Forward of that they curve up in ever sharper radius, though usually the chine line curves up first and more sharply than the keel. As the beam also narrows, the combined effect is to greatly steepen the dead-rise angle of the bow sections.

In his later designs, Grover Loening favored carrying the straight keel line well forward with very little upward curve. He contended that the resulting deeper bow lines were sharper, like a boat, and the force vector when meeting a wave was more backwards than upwards and so disturbed the pitch less. Also, the "finer" entry tended to cleave the waves rather than to push a collar of foam ahead at low speed. The sharp bow of the Dornier DO–X was designed according to this theory. On the other hand, the normal curved bow permits easier debarking onto a beach because of more overhang. It also eases the slight blow when the bow hits a sloping ramp.

The peak of the bow should be just as high as it can be made without intercepting downward vision at the landing angle. If this can be improved by raising the cockpit, that

Dornier DO-X, showing her classic bow lines. (Apparent curve in stem is black part of ornamental bow trim.) (Edward Jablonski)

is a better solution. Engineers who drew rounded bows in profile didn't believe I had seen fish swim by the windshield. The argument raged for years and was only compromised by agreeing we *could* have seen them if the fish had been in those waters.

There is no well-established rule of thumb for proportioning the length of the forebody, except to say it has gradually lengthened in recent years with no disadvantages except for weight and cost. Forward buoyancy, of course, is needed to establish the correct water line.

BOW SECTIONS

This discussion has clearly established the philosophy of bottom design stipulating that water must always flow over flat or concave surfaces, but never over convex surfaces. Except for negligible skin friction, water forces act normal (perpendicular) to the surface over which the water flows. Forces on the bottom will be inward and upward if concave; outward and downward if convex. As shown in figure 13, when the forebody bottom is made with flat sheets, and

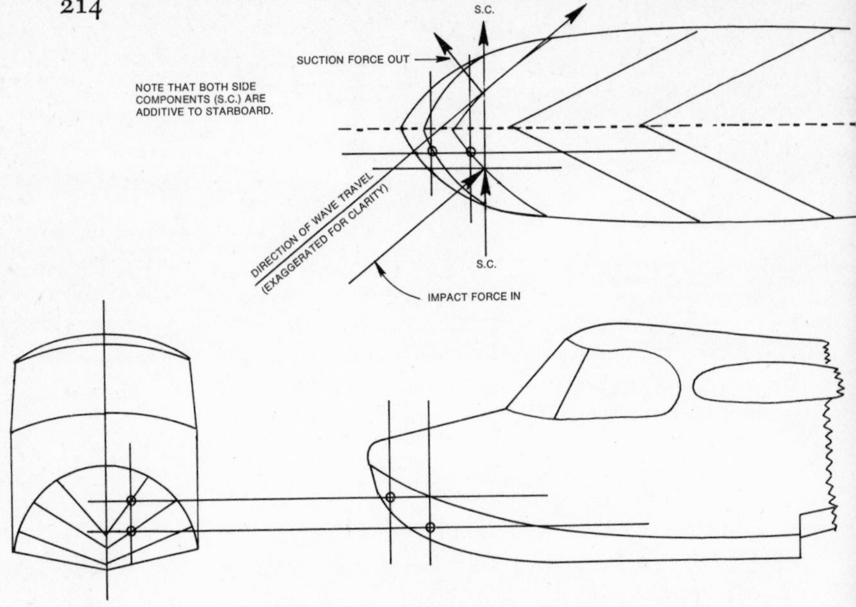

Figure 13—Bow Sections

the angle of dead rise is increased, as usual, in the extreme bow sections, waterlines in that area will be convex. Sideways forces can be produced on the bow conducive to water loops (figure 13).

When such a hull pitches downward slightly at planing speed, and the bow is fully wetted, there is an outward and downward force on each side; no trouble—if they are symmetrical. When, for any reason, the seaplane is yawed, there is inward and sideways force on the advancing side, at the time that convexity creates further outward and sideways force in the same direction on the opposite side. A water loop impends. Once unsymmetrical forces occur and the bow yields, these side forces increase catastrophically. The "direction of wave travel" shown on the diagram may be exaggeratedly acute for the start of a water loop, but it is accurate for a well-developed water loop. In addition, the downward forces will depress the bow still further, moving the center of lateral pressure on the hull so far forward a further swerving moment is added. This unexpected involuntary maneuver occurs so quickly and violently that pilots experiencing it for the first time rarely understand what happened. The design precept calls for concave sections in the extreme bow.

AFTERBODY LINES

At the beginning of this chapter I said that a seaplane could take off and land without any afterbody. That is true in calm water, but the hull needs length behind to bear on the water in rough seas and keep it from pitching wildly. In effect, it provides "wheelbase." It operates in the wake of the main step, and the problem is to keep it planing too. Figure 14 shows the pattern of flow off the main step of a conventional V bottom at about the time the seaplane is

Figure 14—Flow Just Prior to Skipping

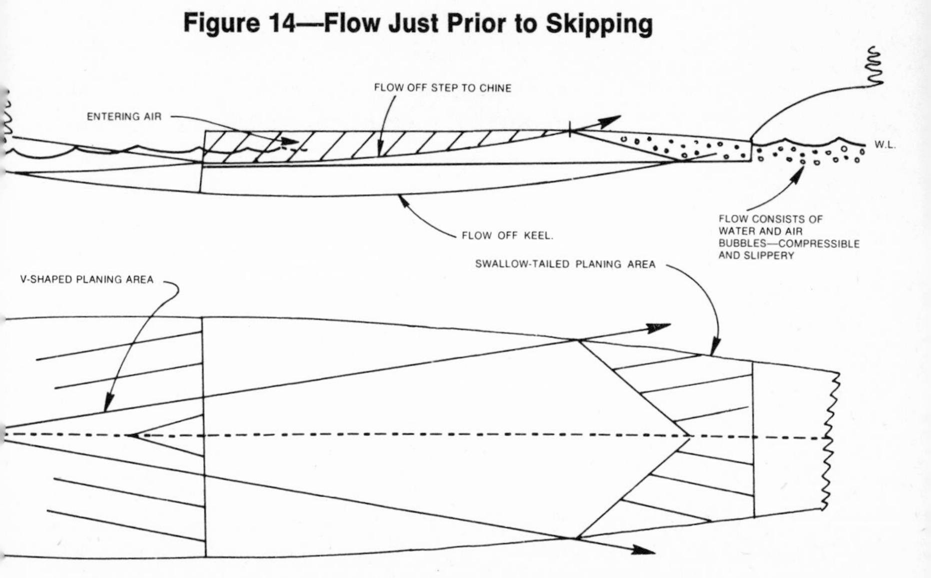

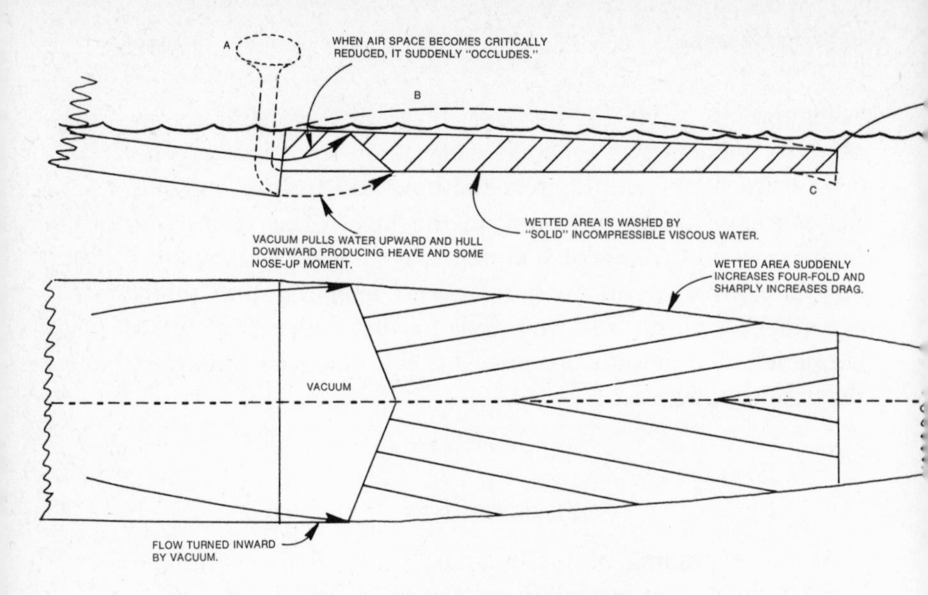

Figure 15—Flow During Skipping

lifting off. The "footprint" at the main step is a V pattern, but it is a swallowtail shape at the rear step. Most of the afterbody is bare because air is flowing in behind the main step, as it should.

Figure 15 shows the flow when the hull momentarily rides deeper as it runs through a wave or is dropped from a height on landing, conditions that induce a skip, as discussed in Part One. The average waterline is now above the main step, "occluding" the afterbody. Little air can flow into the area, and a vacuum is formed, producing the skip. The afterbody is not "ventilated." There are several design alternatives that improve this situation.

The step should be deep. It is pretty hard to increase the depth in a completed seaplane, but if test flights indicate there is no serious change in pitch attitude, the step can be extended aft where it will also be deepened. Then, if the sides of the extension are left open, some relieving air will enter.

Ventilating ducts can introduce air behind the step, indicated by dotted line A. The air intakes should be well above the waterline. Often they breathe through amphibian wheel pockets. Once the air intakes were inside the cabin of a large flying boat, but the pressure change on the crew's ears when she skipped was intolerable.

Warped afterbodies, indicated by dotted line B, have become popular on large flying boats. The angle of dead rise increases sharply behind the main step and is usually decreased toward the rear step, where it is again equal to the dead rise of the forebody, thus restoring a more normal footprint there.

Planing tail body is a term used when the afterstep is as far aft as the very tail, at the rudder post.

V-shaped main steps have several advantages. They allow air to flow more easily under the afterbody, particularly if it is also warped. The point of the step will become deeper than at the chine because it is farther aft. It also provides an easier entry into rough seas when landing.

In the attempt to suppress skipping, there was a period when turned-down, or "hooked" rear steps were popular, indicated by dotted line C. In theory, they provided more lift there, and surely they did—so much so, they were repelled rather than establishing the steady planing support desired. Even when the afterbody was not smothered, a wave could nose the hull down sharply enough to induce a single oscillation somewhat short of a true skip.

England pioneered many of these design refinements, and they were the last hydrodynamic contributions from the National Advisory Committee for Aeronautics before it became the NASA and turned its attention to space flight. The Martin Marlin P5M–16 was the last of the Navy patrol flying boats. The deeper bow keel line, the pointed V main step, the warped chine line, and the planing tail are four of her most obvious characteristics.

One of the nicest amphibian flying boats I ever flew was the Goodyear Aircraft Company's GA–22 in 1950. Water flying would be even more popular today if she had gone into production. (See below.) She could carry four people 750 nautical miles at 105 knots with a 225-horsepower engine. She was a beautiful craft with excellent bottom lines and spray patterns. She resides today in the Museum of the Sport Aviation Association in Hales Corners, Wisconsin. The main step was very deep and pointed with a large fillet behind that fared smoothly into the planing tail afterbody in classic simplicity. Airborne drag under the hull was minimal. I detected no clanking noise underneath. When taxiing at high speed the wetted area of the step narrowed to that of a water ski. Her rough-water behavior was superlative, with a very soft landing entry into high waves. Although more than twenty years have passed, there have been no further hull bottom improvements, with the possible exception of one home-designed sport amphibian under construction and not yet tested.

Goodyear GA-22 four-place Amphibian. She had an excellent 1950 design, but unfortunately, she never went into production. (Goodyear Aircraft)

LATERAL STABILITY

Since the center of gravity of a seaplane is far above the center of buoyancy, capsize must be prevented by auxiliary means. Small floats under the wings and sea wings are the only two methods short of a catamaran.

WING-TIP FLOATS

Lateral support or righting moment is provided equally by small floats at the tips or larger floats near the hull. Both provide buoyancy when the seaplane is at rest, or planing lift when it is taxiing. Usually they are positioned to support the floating seaplane with a 2- to 4-degree list to either side. The position fore and aft is unimportant from the righting viewpoint. They are normally attached to the wing so that the resulting lift and drag forces pass approximately through the torsional center of the wing chord. The forces they apply to the wing are usually below its normal design strength, except that the tip of the wing must be stiffer than normal in torsion.

Wing-tip floats resemble small hulls, though their keel line must be 5 degrees or more above the main keel angle to assure planing lift on any passing wave. Streamlining for air drag results usually in a pointed stern. Float bottoms are V-ed though on small seaplanes they may have the simplicity of flat bottoms. When the floats are long in respect to the wing chord, as would be the case for larger floats placed well inboard, they often have a small step to assure that the planing lift force will not twist the wing excessively. Conventionally, upper decks are rounded in section and profile in the image of the upper wing chord surface above. When crowded completely underwater, as when turning in strong crosswinds, flow over the deck strongly supplements the planing lift.

Floats are supported by a wide variety of strut patterns, or on cantilever pylons. On small airplanes with wings very close to the water, the float may be integral with the wing; that is, the sides extend upward to the wing forming a light, stiff structure. Air drag might be less, but water drag is higher, and the advantage of upper surface lift is lost, though there is more displacement working at slow speed.

SEA WINGS

The advantages claimed for sea wings, often called "sponsons," included extra planing surface in the early stages of takeoff, appreciable air lift from the ground (water) cushion, and perhaps less air drag. They provide a most convenient platform or deck on very large boats where passengers may board and stand up under the wing. It was further claimed they would still operate even if badly bent by high seas that might have completely carried away a wing-tip float, leading to disaster. The fore-and-aft cross section is that of a thick wing, often with a truncated trailing edge and pitched to a high angle of incidence. Sprouting from the hull at the waterline, their flotation is sufficient to assure no heel or list when the ship is at rest. They become even more effective as heavy gross loads raise the waterline.

Behavior of sea wings during takeoff is both helpful and detrimental. At very low speeds there is stiff lateral support. When the bow wave builds up there is a period when its trough passes under the sponson giving little lateral support, and this speed must be avoided when crosswind. Spray off the bow as the hull goes on the step strikes the underside with considerable mass, recapturing more lift. Sponsons are out of the water during high-speed taxiing, though in rough seas there is a period when they take terrific impact.

I never flew a boat with sea wings. I did observe them on the previously mentioned round trip across the Atlantic in a Boeing 314. There was a fresh west wind blowing as we taxied out from LaGuardia Airport under the Whitestone Bridge. Captain Harold Gray, who later became president of Pan American, made the downwind turn pretty gingerly and continued slowly enough so the bow wave trough was not under the sponson. I worried about the upwind turn, and sure enough, the whole starboard wing tip of that giant airplane went into the water, greatly alarming the passengers. It had been anticipated, and cabin attendants were posted to tell us to "think nothing of it"! The ship recovered without trouble and idled into the wind a long time while water drained out of scuppers in the trailing edge. We later learned the time was needed for the three crew members who had been sent out into the tunnel of the upwind wing to crawl back in. They provided ballast, though it had proved insufficient. Meanwhile, water that had flowed into the bridge deck from the downwind tunnel was pumped out of the bilge. The wind assisted in a surprisingly short takeoff with liftoff just as we passed under the bridge.

On the return flight, when we landed at Horta in the Azores, the seas were high. The landing with reduced fuel load was innocuous, barring the usual heavy bottom pounding. I was interested to see that the big hull decelerated with little pitch though all was obscured in clouds of flying spray. While we refueled and the passengers all trooped up to a little hostelry for rare Portuguese wines, there was long discussion on the dock, as I listened, on whether Captain Marius Lodeesen should attempt a takeoff or hold over for calmer seas. Often there were week-long delays during the first year of transatlantic flight. The Captain told us he would make an experimental run and then determine whether we would return for holdover or make the actual takeoff.

I scrambled aboard before the others and took the seat on the port side with the window right at the leading edge of the sea wing. The huge ship felt heavy with fuel and "logy" as we taxied out behind the shelter of the breakwater. There was a two-mile stretch ahead parallel to the shore terminating in a high cape. The wind was moderately on our port, though the seas, which had bent around the cape, were dead ahead. Almost immediately, we started with full power and there was nothing to see but rushing white water outside the window. Then the series of thumps and shudders as the seas struck the sea wings were appalling. Finally, as the speed increased, we could see through the spray along the sides of the hull and observe the sponsons, although the jarring continued unabated. I learned in college physics classes that water is incompressible. That day we had the proof. The great combers would rush toward us and impact under the sea wing and immediately *reverse* and come gushing out far ahead of the hull only to be blown back over the ship in a welter of rainbows.

It appeared we could get off before the cape, though the waves were becoming even higher. However, Lodeesen throttled down until he could see the conditions off the cape. He settled off the step when the waves were more nearly abeam, cautiously executed the port turn through the eye of the wind, and taxied back. He reported he was satisfied, and we would go. Closer to the shore on that takeoff, we repeated the first run. It seemed again we would be airborne before the cape, but to our surprise he throttled down somewhat as we approached the place where the waves were highest and still nearly head on. As we passed the cape and the seas and wind were almost abeam on our port, he gunned the four engines and bore off in a gradual offwind turn that put us right along the crest of a big swell. We planed into the air with ease.

The only recent flying boat with sea wings is a small home-built designed by M.V. (Mort) Taylor. His sponsons continue out and become the wings with sharp dihedral. He calls them "float wings." There are no trailing edge flaps. If rough water and high wind were not a consideration, we might see other flying boats with wings very close to the water. I was associated in the design of a small, three-passenger flying boat with wings that seemed alarmingly low. I worried that the trailing edge of the aileron might dig under when she was drifting backwards in a strong wind without power, perhaps leading to a capsize.

We wore life preservers when we tested her in a 30-knot wind, moving into rougher water on each landing. We were careful to keep the flaps up. The wing offered no trouble even though we attained her limit in rough water. So we cut the engine and remained alert to see what happened. Her weathercocking stability held her head into the wind, although her backward speed must have been a good eight knots. Then one of us crawled out a way on the wing to depress the tip into the water, while holding full up-aileron. The wing tip dug under and went down a lot farther, while the wing man scrambled back in. But the drag was so great, the plane yawed sharply and promptly lifted the wing tip out. If either the aileron or the flaps had been down, they would probably have been folded under. We guessed the low wing position was OK but would never wish to see a lower one.

Flying boat design is far more complicated than landplane design and every contingency that can occur on the water must be considered during the original layout.

18

PROPELLER LOCATION

Locating engines and propellers to protect them from spray, cabin entrance doors, and many other problems must be considered in the original layout. One cannot work on the engine by standing on water! Fuel drains must go overboard and not through the bottom. Oil drips must never get inside the hull. Provision for stowage of marine equipment is essential. If such minor items are overlooked by the designer, they will be expensive to rectify when the plane is completed.

PROPELLER LOCATIONS

The simple tractor nose propeller of the landplane is obviously out of the question; it must go on top somewhere. Assuming the propeller is attached directly to the engine without an extended drive shaft or transmission, a tractor nacelle on struts may be located over the bow. Or the prop may be behind the cabin over the wing, or between the wings if on a biplane, and may then be either a tractor or a pusher.

The farther forward, the freer the prop is from spray. But then, in order to balance the airplane, the cabin moves aft under the wing, and the prop becomes a fence between cabin and dock, even assuming an easy exit door can be contrived. When the cabin is as large as a Fleet Wings Sea Bird or a Grumman Widgeon, the solution is a nose compartment reached from inside and opening to a deck hatch ahead of the prop. This hatch should be hinged at the back as a shield between bowman and the prop disc. The required inside crawl space eliminates the whole right side of the instrument panel and is awkward for large people. Small flying boats naturally tend to put the cabin forward and the prop aft.

Excessive noise and vibration occur in the plane of a spinning prop. To reduce this, the recent trend in twin-engine landplanes increases the space between the prop tips and the sides of the cabin to at least a foot. If the nacelle of a single-engine boat is placed as a tractor above the wing, the prop turns above the highest part of the hull, and must be further raised to reduce noise. The thrust line height becomes excessive, so a pusher nacelle, farther aft and lower, is often favored for small flying boats.

The wing shelters the prop disc from spray. In the interest of a fast, clean hull, the designer would like to place the wing at the level of the cabin roof with the further advantage of getting it well above the waterline. In the interest of compactness, he wishes to lower the nacelle and prop. There are three vertical dimensions that must be reduced to the minimum and preferably should not be additive: depth of hull, depth of cabin, height of thrust line. One solution is to lower the prop until it turns just above the low after hull deck. The cabin lines fair rearward very sharply to a vertical, but blunt, knife-edge ahead of the prop. Then the wing, engine, and prop are on the level of the cabin roof. The prop is poorly shielded from flying spray.

Republic Sea Bee on land.

When the goal of keeping the thrust line low is abandoned, the engine can go above on a "stalk." Or alternatively, every effort can be made to fair the flow over the cabin both downward and inward. No surfaces should curve inward so sharply that the flow breaks away and becomes turbulent in front of the prop disc. 'Tis a puzzlement.

One method must be avoided because it badly stalls out the center section during a power-off approach. It seems logical to place the wing low so the prop swings above the trailing edge, and to fair the cabin lines into a vertical knife-edge with the nacelle atop the cabin roof. It appears that airflow over the wing and inward behind the cabin will be smooth. However, such flow is no more than moderately favorable even at cruising speed when the prop is pulling air into the disc. When the propeller stops thrusting or has to windmill at idling power, the flow goes all to pieces. The cubic foot of air that passes over the deepest part of the wing chord, next to the vertical cabin side, has to follow simultaneously downward over the rest of the wing surface and inward over the back end of the cabin. It refuses. It is asked to expand, which it cannot do. The streamline flow breaks down. A stalled area spreads far out the trailing edge and over the entire end of the cabin.

As the wing approaches a high angle of attack for landing, the stall becomes worse. Effectiveness of the tail surfaces is reduced. Although lifting flow over the outer area of the wing may remain satisfactory, each half wing now has a very low effective aspect ratio. Lift distribution over the whole wing is no longer uniform. The approach angle is very steep. Landing flare must be quick and accurate lest she "go through the bottom." No amount of smooth filleting will solve the problem, because it would be cut off abruptly in front of the prop disc, making a large dead-air area. Vibration is bad, to say nothing of the loss in thrust. We know—we've tried it!

When the wing is set high on the cabin roof and the thrust line is just a bit higher, as on the Sea Bee, there is smooth airflow over the upper surface of the wing and relatively smooth inward airflow below the wing behind the widest part of the cabin. The downward and inward flows are now separated and combine behind the cabin, wing, and prop without serious stalling effects. However, they leave two large trailing vortices that are energy-consuming and inimical to a fast airplane.

PUSHER PROPELLERS

The whole dynamic pattern of pusher props deserves discussion. The argument over the merits of tractors and pushers has raged since airplanes first flew, and is still seething. Proponents of pushers say it is illogical to submerge all parts of the fuselage and wing roots in a tractor slipstream. Drag must be greatly increased because the airflow is some 15 percent greater than the rest of the airplane and contains pulsating turbulence. Proponents of tractors say that pushers operate in distorted airflow, are noisy, and prevent good nose-to-tail streamlining. Also, in many installations the engine requires special internal flow considerations to cool adequately, though there is no evidence that cooling drag is necessarily more than a tractor.

The hottest argument boiled around the reputed pusher decrease in thrust efficiency. Then the Cessna center-line-thrust Skymaster Model 337, dubbed the "Mixmaster," appeared. A landplane, it has a tractor in the nose and a pusher at the end of a short fuselage. Two cantilever tail booms from the wings support the tail. To the humiliation of the tractor boosters, she climbed faster and had a higher single-engine ceiling on the rear engine! Now the furor is nearly over. In the interest of the Cessna Company, and as a boon to the tractor adherents, it should be added that the 1972 pressurized Skymaster adjusted and refined cooling drags, and used a slightly larger diameter front prop, resulting in equal single-engine performance front and rear.

PUSHER DESIGN DETAILS

There are tricks to designing aircraft with pusher engines. The airflow in front of the prop should be streamlined with extra care. Any turbulence entering the disc is a source of noise. The next time you fly in a small pusher, open the cabin window and put out your arm. The resulting turbulence will noticeably increase the sound level. But don't lose your glove in the slipstream! A soft glove won't hurt the prop, but small nuts and bolts perhaps jarred off the cowling will. The loss of a cabin door or piece of cowling might be disastrous. Design all details accordingly. Exhaust pipes may discharge into the prop disc with only slight increase in noise and soot on the blades, but it is better to diffuse the exhaust.

Propellers may be moderately yawed to the airstream with slight loss in efficiency. Nevertheless, when a tractor prop is close to the leading edge of the wing and operates in the advancing upwash, both the thrust and wing airflow will be improved if the thrust line is pointed down a few degrees. Pusher propellers operate in the downwash flow behind the wing and will give maximum thrust when the thrust line is set parallel to the flow, pointing downward to the rear. A rule-of-thumb method says the combined over-and-under airflow off a wing is parallel to the bisector of the two surfaces at the trailing edge. A few experimental landplanes have buried engines in the trailing edge of the wing and have made the mistake of not canting the thrust line downward. A thrust line parallel to the center line turns the downwash back up, thus decreasing the total lift. When the shaft line on trailing edge installations is at the trailing edge level, a two-bladed prop will shudder. Both blades pass through the slow boundary layer wake simultaneously. If the thrust line is moderately above the trailing edge, though still angled down, the blades slice through the boundary wake more smoothly. A three-bladed prop would be still smoother.

As mentioned earlier, the Piaggio Company of Italy developed an appealing twin-engine amphibian, assembled and marketed in the United States by Kearny-Trecker as the Royal Gull. The wings were "gulled"; that is, the center section had a steep dihedral to a "knuckle," then bent to an outboard section with no dihedral. It served to raise the thrust line, the engines being mounted on the upper surface of the wing at the knuckle. The propellers were pushers, and the discs cut deeply into the spray blisters during the entire takeoff. It was a nice amphibian that just missed a big market, probably because of this one weakness. Many thought she was the concept of a landplane designer. This may have been true, because when the hull was changed to a fuselage, she sold well in Europe for several years as a simple landplane.

I had an enjoyable half day of flying the Gull. The noise level was acceptable for her day, but had a puzzling sort of buzz that seemed to penetrate the whole ship. I finally attributed this to the battering the props were putting into the wing ahead of them. They turned as close to the trailing edge as the width of the prop blade. There are strong pulsations in the flow immediately ahead of a prop. Any part of the structure should be at least three or more prop blade-widths ahead of the working part of the blade. Clearance is less important nearer the hub, where the blades are thicker, and in the wake of the engine. The first configuration of the previously mentioned experimental amphibian had a cabin terminating in a long vertical slot intended to assist cooling. It was very close to the wooden propeller. I expected the cowling would soon crack under the beating. It didn't. In four hours of test flying there was a large crack in the prop blade instead! Keep them well separated.

LONGITUDINAL FLIGHT TRIM

High thrust lines obviously produce a strong nose-down moment. It is balanced by a greater down load on the stabilizer, achieved either by more area or more down angle. An equivalent loss in total lift results, which is the major penalty of high thrust lines. When the throttle is suddenly closed, the plane will nose up abruptly, usually assuming a correct glide angle, without much stabilizer trim change, when the cruise speed decays. Or, if gunned in a glide, the nose initially dives before increasing speed restores the trim. Since a pusher prop is well aft, the tail is deeply immersed in the slipstream and becomes more sensitive to sudden changes. On the other hand, it is less affected by rough air, and the airplane flies more smoothly. When the pusher thrust line points well downward onto the stabilizer, there is more self-correction. Sudden reduction in nose-down thrust is better balanced by the sudden change in slipstream velocity.

There is reason to fear that an engine mounted on struts or a stalk above and behind the cabin will plunge into it from a crash with a nose-low impact. In the old days, "Sampson" struts ran from the engine nacelle to the bow to protect the occupants in that type of crash. Modern designers should strengthen engine stalks for the same purpose, though, of course, a severe crash might cause equally severe injuries from crushing forces through the bow.

OTHER PROPELLER LOCATIONS

Locating twin- or four-engine props in the leading edges is now practically standard. Twin nacelles above the wings no longer appear even on very small boats, possibly because as RPM has increased, smaller-diameter props are in vogue. When twin floats are installed under twin-engine landplanes, the props turn closely over the forward float decks. Dangerous acrobatics by crew members prevail in attaining the forward decks for docking or anchoring purposes. A few seaplanes have placed engines in the hull with remote drive shafts to the prop. They suffer from cabin noise and odor, inaccessibility and extra transmission weight and cost. Unless kept scrupulously clean, the engine might be a fire hazard.

Tandem engines in one nacelle were once popular and relatively efficient. The after prop works in the slipstream of the front prop, requiring higher blade pitch to compensate for the faster inflow. A very fast, large Dornier flying boat, the DO–26, had four engines in two long tandem nacelles snug to the top of the wing. The front props turned ahead of the leading edge, and the rear props behind the trailing edge, where they would be subject to severe beating from spray off the hull. To prevent this, the whole after end of the nacelles, including the rear engine and prop, hinged upward perhaps 20 degrees, enough for the after prop tips to be higher than the trailing edges, and thus protected during the takeoff. The resulting thrust down-load from the shaft hinged at an angle to the airflow was considered an acceptable penalty offsetting the drag of raised nacelles.

Many combinations of tractor and pushers have been tried on large multiengine flying boats. The NC–4 type used a central tandem nacelle with two outboard tractor nacelles. In World War II the Germans had a flying boat whose purpose was to protect small shipping in the North Sea. She had a single tractor prop and two pusher wing nacelles with swiveling machine guns in the noses. An excellent Latecoere six-engine boat had two tandem inboard nacelles with outboard nacelles each containing a single tractor. That was the ship with wing-tip floats retracting against the bottom of the outboard nacelles.

The small amphibian problems of prop location, cabin doors, forward deck access, and flow ahead of the prop are all closely related. Spray strips at the chine have been described. Some boats, even large ones, have added auxiliary spray strips parallel to the center line forward and below the windshield to retard the spray that may obscure vision during takeoff. Such a strip may be used as a side deck to reach the bow for anchoring. A current amphibian under development which grapples with all these problems most successfully is the Griswold Polyphibian, designed by Roger W. Griswold II. It has excellent doors on both sides, side walk-rail-spray-strips, and a large anchor hatch, as well as ingenious wing-tip floats, and smooth cabin lines in front of the prop, though they are still divergent toward the trailing edge.

SPRAY—AGAIN

Stabilizers should be placed as high above water as practical. T tails are becoming popular. They make special sense for flying boats. The poor tail surfaces naturally take the worst beating from spray—they get it all. More large boats in air-sea-rescue operations have suffered elevator and stabilizer damage than wing-tip float damage.

Photographs of flying boats about 100 feet high after takeoff always show water still blowing off all parts of the aircraft. Droplets adhering to any surface offer a lot of drag. All pilots have noticed the decrease in speed when flying through rain. Amphibian water takeoffs usually require more run and more time than the same airplane on land, becoming airborne at a slightly higher speed. Prop RPM, and hence horsepower, with fixed pitch props, is noticeably lower until all the droplets are whirled off.

19

OTHER DESIGN CONSIDERATIONS

ADDITIONAL FIN AREA

A side view of any floatplane shows the bows of the floats projecting far forward. The center of pressure from side forces, as in a sideslip, lies much farther ahead than when the same plane is flown on wheels. Since the floats are double, they have a double effect in diminishing the normal straightening effect of the vertical tail surfaces. More vertical tail area is required. If it is not added, some floatplanes will even "bite their own tails"; a sideslip with free controls will actually increase until the plane yaws off into a spin.

In the late twenties my first true experimental test flying was on my own Kitty Hawk, when we first mounted one on Edo floats. It was in the days when "flat-spins" were giving test pilots gray hairs. Some experimental airplanes would become locked in a fast, flat, nose-up spin from which they were unable to recover. After establishing the spin, the test pilot would free the stick and watch to see if it would move full aft of its own accord. This meant the elevator had gone full up, and the spin was going flat. It behooved him to push forward to recover—darned quick.

I designed the Kitty Hawk with a relatively long tail and with "decalage" in the biplane wings. That is, the upper forward wing had a degree and a half more angle of attack than the lower wing staggered farther aft. The upper stalled first and pitched the nose down. Also, she had a modern radial engine in a short nose, thus compacting the fore-and-aft weight distribution. These features, coupled with a restricted up-elevator, made her one of the very few airplanes rated by the Aeronautics Branch of the Department of Commerce (FAA ancestor) as "characteristically incapable of spinning." In fact, in order to teach tailspins to students, we had to give one ship in each school more up-elevator to achieve a spin at all.

The Kitty Hawk seaplane had enough original vertical tail area to straighten herself out of a sideslip, though rather slowly. But I was most disappointed to find she had true flat-spinning tendencies. I had to recover in time after eight or ten turns before she really went flat. Once I was almost too late. As on almost every floatplane, more vertical area was needed.

Usually supplemental fins are added on floatplane conversions. These may be ventral fins added to the fuselage under the tail, or they may be a pair of small auxiliary vertical fins added above and below the stabilizer near the tips. We discarded these fixes because they would mar the beauty of our little ship. We found it simpler to substitute a complete new and taller fin and rudder to add the requisite area on each seaplane conversion. With them, she spun and recovered normally and was better coordinated in level flight. However, Kitty Hawk seaplanes would fall out of a stall into a spin, though none ever did spin in.

AUXILIARY PLANING SURFACES

Hydrofoils and water skis may be used below a hull to provide auxiliary lift. Hydrofoils, like an airplane wing, have a large span and narrow chord with aspect ratios of at least six, and often much more. They provide lift either from an airfoil section or from a wedge section with cut-off trailing edge known as a "supercavitating foil." Water skis are long on the fore and aft axis and very narrow. Although the upper surface is usually curved, it is far from an airfoil section. As soon as the seaplane passes the hump, skis plane on the top of the water with no solid flow over the upper surface like a foil. Both types have negligible displacement; they provide no buoyancy. (See page 141.)

HYDROFOILS

In England in 1861, Thomas Moy patented a hydrofoil and demonstrated it by towing a foil-equipped small boat until "it lifted completely out of the water." Not until 1912 did airplane wings again develop as good a foil section. Most of the early attempts to fly off water were made with hydrofoils of many patterns, and even Fabre's first successful seaplane used a sort of "foil-float." The Wright Brothers made full-scale tests of hydrofoils in Dayton in 1907, but were called to France before they could continue plans for making a hydrofoil seaplane.

Development of hydrofoils for surface vessels has continued, until today quite large ships are foil-borne. The US Navy has sponsored flight tests by the Edo Corporation and the Thurston Aircraft Corporation on hydrofoil seaplanes with a view to improving deep-sea operations. Both series of tests confirm that the addition of foils to a flying boat greatly improved rough-water capability by reducing landing shocks on the whole aircraft, and by reducing hull bottom loading too. Operation in seas approximately 40 percent higher than the normal hull limitation seemed attainable. Weight saved by reducing bottom stress was theoretically more than the weight of the foil and retracting mechanism.

When the hull is perched on struts high above the planing foil, it is unstable about all axes. It is essential that the foil not "unport" before the speed of full aerodynamic control. That is, it should remain submerged during part of the take-off. When it unports there is a momentary spectacular burst of spray below the hull. It looked bad in photographs, so tests were made to determine the micron size of the droplets.

Unlike the solid spray from the hull, the tested droplets were hardly larger than those of fog. Even so, the test pilot grumbled, "there was a hell of a lot of fog."

Of course, a seaplane cannot be handled in shallow water or brought ashore unless the foils are retractable, a sufficient complication to prevent any practical use to date, but certainly not an insurmountable problem.

WATER SKIS

Water skis under a hull function the same as hydrofoils. They ease entry into rough water and reduce bottom loading from wave impacts. A number of installations have been made under Navy contract and by civilian experimenters with results nearly the same as hydrofoils. Perhaps retraction methods are a bit simpler. They may be less vulnerable to driftwood when planing. Like hydrofoils, they have never yet appeared on any production seaplane.

Reference was made in the History Section to the Convair Sea Dart jet-powered fighter. She flew well, and four were built, but she was not the match of a landplane fighter in combat. The profile photo (page 238) shows her general arrangement. The two skis had the same curve as the hull bottom and folded forward into flush grooves. The photo on page 239 shows her taxiing at slow speed. When she was at rest, the waterline was not far below the cockpit. The Delta wings provided lateral stability, before the skis unported.

Convair Sea Dart with retractable shock-absorbing water skis. (General Dynamics)

In one stage of tests, she had a single water ski installed under the center line also retracting into a curved groove in the fuselage. The plan form of this ski was a triangle, quite wide at the bow and tapering nearly to a point at the heel.

During the fifties the All America Company removed the landing gear from a standard small Stinson landplane and mounted it on a pair of water skis with struts long enough to allow the propeller to turn above the water when planing. There was no flotation of any sort. For several months many pilots flew it from a wooden ramp on the lower Delaware River. The plane slid down the ramp on the skis, attaining planing speed before entering the water. As long as the speed was kept above 20 mph she taxied well and took off and landed easily. If a slower speed had ever been attempted, she would have settled off the skis and sunk. Upon return, she contacted the wet ramp with a moderate jar and taxied to the apron.

At that time, inflatable helicopter floats mounted on top of the skids were not developed. In the forties, the McKinley

Pneumatic Float Company mounted several Cubs on inflated planing floats. With a streamlined shape, heavy fabric reinforcement where the struts attached, and inflated side tubes to make hard chines, they were in service at least one summer at a Long Island seaplane base. It was said internal air pressure was higher than usual to hold the planing bottom shape. Probably they would be practical only on very light airplanes.

Someone someday is going to attach air bags to the top of water skis, and a lightweight, low-drag seaplane may result. In flight, the collapsed bags would nestle into a tray on top of the ski, offering little drag. After landing and while still planing, an electric air compressor would inflate the bags, and the seaplane could settle onto their flotation to dock or moor like any other seaplane. Battery power would actuate

Convair Sea Dart taxiing at slow speed. The delta wing tips needed no wing tip floats. (General Dynamics)

the compressor when air pressure dropped below normal during the night. The bags must be streamlined enough to permit attaining ski-unporting speed, after which the compressor would be reversed to suck out the air and collapse the bags before takeoff.

VERTICAL FLOATS

When scientists wish to measure wave heights with extreme accuracy, they prefloat a large, heavy spar buoy with depth graduations, and observe the difference from crest to trough. The inertia is so great the buoy moves up and down almost imperceptibly as waves pass, and holds steady at the average half height.

In order to listen underwater for enemy submarines, the Navy would like to land carrier-based, short-range helicopters and long-range, shore-based verticraft at sea. Conceivably, they might remain out there on station for several days. Experiments were made with a small copter on four "spar buoy" floats. In cruise configurations the copter appeared to have a pair of normal, but rather slim, floats, each supported bow and stern by a pair of cantilever struts. While hovering before landing, each half-float rotated around the bottom of the struts into a vertical position. Landings and takeoffs in a very rough sea were no problem.

Then the Navy made three large vertical floats to support a Martin "Mariner" patrol plane with the hull high above the water. For the tests it was towed slowly out into a large swell, and a standard "Mariner" landed nearby, just barely escaping high-sea damage. The floating behavior of both was to be studied from a standby vessel for several hours. Within fifteen minutes the least seasick crew member of the standard flying boat staggered to the microphone and reported conditions were intolerable. They were taking off and the hell with it, or words to that effect. So they woke up the peacefully slumbering crew on the vertical floats and everyone went home! If the Navy pursues this mission with verticraft, vertical floats may appear.

AIR CUSHION LANDING GEAR

In recent years, Great Britain has led Canada and the United States in the development of air cushion vehicles. England calls them hovercraft. Originally, the United States called them "GEMS" for Ground Effect Machines. Now the popular terms are "ACVs" for Air Cushion Vehicles, or "SESs" for Surface Effect Ships. Whatever the name, the basic concept provides air lubrication under a hull. This "new concept" has surprising antiquity, and at least this development had American sponsorship. In 1863, an humble Hudson River ferryboat nicknamed the *Smoothing Iron* introduced compressed air through longitudinal underwater strips providing air-bubble lubrication. It worked! She used less power to attain the same speed as her rival ferries, until the power for the air compressor was added, and then the total power of both was equal. More recently, the thirst for high water speeds and the availability of great thrust from air propellers has put the principle into practical use for surface vessels. Powerful blowers supply air to a large air cushion under the whole hull.

I have ridden aboard an ACV ten miles offshore in a sea state of low three (waves three feet high) and have slid in and out of the water over grassy flats in the St. Lawrence River at 55 mph. There is firm promise this concept could produce a universal landing gear for flying boats capable of operating on quite rough water and rough unprepared fields. The secret lies in the "skirts" that contain the underneath air cushion. A peripheral curtain of tough reinforced fabric floats the whole aircraft on the captured air bubble with suitable internal provisions for stability. Air escapes in a thin sheet under the hem of the skirt. The skirt brushes across waves and hummocks with little drag. Although more air escapes, it is constantly restored by the blowers.

When the craft is at rest, the air blows a hole or depression in the water whose displacement is equal to the gross weight of the craft. At high speed, this depression has to have the same displacement, but then its dimensions are the wide beam multiplied by great length produced by speed. The depth of the depression then becomes very thin. Only ripples appear in the wake in calm water. The effect is analogous to running fast over thin ice to prevent breaking through.

In 1973, a twin-engine DeHaviland Buffalo was modified for an air-cushion landing gear. The peripheral skirt containing the air bubble is a tube inflated by an air compressor. When the compressor is reversed it sucks all the air out of the tube and neatly "retracts" the gear. To make the concept practical, the airplane must land and take off without undergoing rotation to a nose-up attitude. So the aircraft was further modified with special high-lift leading-edge devices that provide maximum landing lift while remaining nearly level. It is too early to assess the worth of this experiment.

WATER RUDDERS

Water rudders are essential. Usually, they are retractable to prevent land or bottom damage. All Edo floats have retractable rudders with an ingenious shape that hinges them upwards should the heel of the float strike a ramp or the bottom even without forward motion. On flying boats, when the rudder post is as low as the static waterline, rudders often retract into the bottom of the air rudder and are actuated by the standard rudder controls. Often, there are springs in the connecting cables to reduce snatch from feedback to the rudder pedals from wave action. When an exposed water rudder is really vulnerable to water or bottom damage, there should be a break-free link in the control so the air rudder cannot be fouled by a bent water rudder. A rudder may be hinged directly from deep-pointed rear steps where it is protected by the afterbody keel line when retracted.

AMPHIBIAN LANDING GEARS

Determining the best way to retract amphibian landing gears brings out the designer's ingenuity. Small amphibs do not usually house the wheels inside but merely rotate them up out of the water. Larger amphibs usually retract the gears out of the airstream into the hull or wings. The many methods of retraction defy classification. Unlike landplanes, sea wings or inboard floats offer convenient structures from which to hinge the gears or even house them within.

Oleo shock struts undergo water submersion satisfactorily, but occasional attention is needed to keep the exposed section bright and clean. The simplicity of spring-type landing gear arms have a special amphibian appeal. Retracting wheels into the bottom of amphibian floats has the advantage of very short legs, though the fourth wheel and its swiveling struts add extra weight and cost. In order to keep the height of a converted landplane low on its wheels, a couple of designs rotated the floats sideways and upwards exposing nonretractable wheels. Some designers have been surprised to find the forces on the operating linkages required to sink the inflated tires are often greater than raising them in the air. Retracting wheels through the hull bottom requires very strong closing doors, and should be avoided.

In 1935, Edo Aircraft built a very fast amphibian to the design and order of Alexander Seversky. She set several

Seversky Amphibian with wheels extended, over New York. (Edo Aircraft)

world amphibian speed records. The main wheels did retract through the bottom successfully. The after ends of the twin floats were raised to make landings on land, using a conventional tail wheel on the fuselage. She was so clean she became the prototype of the Republic Thunderbolt fighters, marking one time when an humble amphibian took the lead in high-performance design.

SIZE RELATIONSHIPS

Most seaplane missions requiring aircraft between 2000 and 7500 pounds are fulfilled equally well by floatplanes or flying boats. Each type has its special features noted throughout this book. Choice of type is decided more by practical mission application than by performance or cost. The larger the aircraft, the fewer built. By overlooking the hordes of DC–3s (or C–47s) produced during World War II, we marvel that Boeing 727 orders now exceed one thousand. It amazes people not familiar with general aviation to learn that Cessna has delivered well over twenty thousand personal size airplanes of *one model* alone. Relatively low cost is an outgrowth of large production, one of the basic advantages of floatplanes over flying boats. The relative advantages of both types vary in three size groups.

Below 2000 pounds, flying boat hulls are very small with little freeboard. Spray patterns may be the same as for larger boats, but little waves become proportionately larger and raise operating problems. Water seems forever to get into the cabin one way or another. There are many advantages in the twin-float configuration for this size airplane. Cabins are high above water, and seats, charts, and instruments keep relatively dry and free of tracked-in sand.

In the bracket of *2000 to 7500 pounds*, there are large overlapping considerations in selecting an optimum type. Great advantage lies in buying a refined up-to-date high-performance landplane and adding the floats, whether they be with or without landing gear. In this size group, a well-designed flying boat will have the edge in performance. The hull-type amphibian will be lower to the ground and more at home on rough airports, particularly in crosswind. The floatplane owner has the ability to rapidly convert for an even higher speed and payload by swapping floats with the regular landing gear. Many owners make the conversion each spring and fall. The initial cost of corrosion-proofing a new landplane and mounting it on amphibious floats brings the final price about equal to that of the boat amphibian, even though the latter has never yet had the cost advantage of a production run exceeding one thousand.

The Grumman Goose and the Beechcraft Model 18 were contemporary at a gross weight of 8000. Each was powered with two Pratt and Whitney Wasp 450-horsepower engines. The floatplane version of the Beech carried a shade more payload than the Goose, though the latter's payload exceeded the Beech when relieved of the weight of the amphibian gear. "Geese" often operate in Alaska as pure seaplanes. You can bet most owners retained the gear, however, and the Beech 18 was never offered with amphibious floats. Fewer than five hundred Geese were delivered. No more than twelve Beechcraft seaplanes ever flew, though more than three thousand landplanes were delivered. Today, a good used Goose commands thrice the resale value of an equivalent Beech.

The smaller twin-engine Grumman Widgeon grossed 4500 pounds, though newer, more powerful engines later installed in most Widgeons raised the performance and gross weight with little increase in payload. A newly overhauled thirty-year-old Widgeon now sells for about the same as an equivalent larger Goose, indicating the demand for the smaller, more popular size. Furthermore, the overhauled thirty-year-old Widgeon sells for about the same as a new, single-engine float amphibian carrying the same payload.

From this pattern of data, the reader may draw his own conclusions and probably justify most any preconceived belief! Out of it, I draw one crystal clear conclusion: It's a seething shame that the present personal airplane market has so few amphibians available.

Above 7500 pounds the flying boat, whether pure seaplane or amphibian, is considered a better aircraft than a floatplane. Toward the end of World War II, a Douglas DC–3 was converted to a floatplane on Edo amphibious floats. To board the airplane from land, passengers climbed up the side of the huge floats, walked aft to a rudimentary ladder up to

Douglas DC-3 on Edo amphibious floats. (Edo Aircraft)

the trailing edge, thence to the wing and into the cabin through a side hatch. The engines were the same as the contemporary PBY–5 Catalina. Although not precisely equal, the two aircraft carried, in short-haul operations, about the same payload, at the same cruising speed, for about the same range. The one DC–3 flew a year or so; there are still PBYs flying today.

So, after all these design variations, it seems everything's been done before, but a lot of good ideas have perished before a little more refinement would have proved their worth. Leroy Grumman was a great designer. He often reminded his engineers that every improvement made in an existing airplane made it carry less, or fly slower, or cost more. And it does! Nevertheless, there is always progress. Better seaplanes will come from brand new designs.

20

MATERIALS AND STRUCTURES

MATERIALS

Seaplane structural materials include aluminum alloys, marine plywood, and fiberglass. Aluminum alloy, known as duralumin, is the standard. Plywood is still popular with home builders. Fiberglass remains too heavy for the basic structure, though it is now almost standard for cowlings, wing tips, fairings, and small lightly loaded components requiring double curvature. Compartments in hulls and floats are often stiffened by filling with a foamed plastic such as styrofoam. Stainless steel is known to be a light durable material, but its cost proved unacceptable. As yet, no ferro cement hulls have appeared; lightweight cement fillers used to cover the wire screens are an interesting possibility.

Aluminum alloys have a strength-to-weight ratio exceeding most steels. They are durable, easily worked, and available in a variety of forms from sheet to extruded sections. 7075–T6 has a yield strength of 60,000 pounds per square inch. Lesser strengths are available for parts needing high ductility. Pure aluminum is too soft for a basic structural material, though it is very corrosion resistant. Alloys of aluminum are affected by salt water and are supplied as

Alclad, an alloy with a very thin coating of pure aluminum. During fabrication this material is either anodized or alodined by dipping each piece in a preservative solution, then priming it with zinc chromate or an epoxy before painting. Parts are joined by riveting or bolting.

Wooden structures are built up almost exclusively from marine glued plywood. Double curved surfaces are simulated by fillets and small fairing blocks. Seams are joined with epoxy glues and Everdur screws. Corrosion is no problem, though interior surfaces should be varnished and exterior surfaces should be painted every year. When steel or alloy fittings face the wood, they should be bedded in a compound to prevent the wood acids from corroding the metal. When wooden seaplanes are kept afloat for long periods, they absorb a moderate weight of water with corresponding reduction in payload.

If *stainless steel* were less expensive, both as a material and in its manufacture, it would be very popular in seaplane construction. It was used exclusively on the Fleet Wings Sea Birds made in the thirties. Two are still flying, looking as new as the day they were completed, even though the hulls have never been painted. The very strong skins were assembled with seam welding for water tightness and were so thin, they left a ripply-appearing surface. The ripples were masked with a whirl finish that still gleams in the sunlight. No aluminum alloy could match their light weight. When landing on rippled water, the bottom sheets filled the cabin with tinkling oriental music.

STRUCTURES

Seaplane wing and tail construction is the same as on a landplane, but hulls differ from fuselages because the bottom receives high water loads and must be watertight. Bare

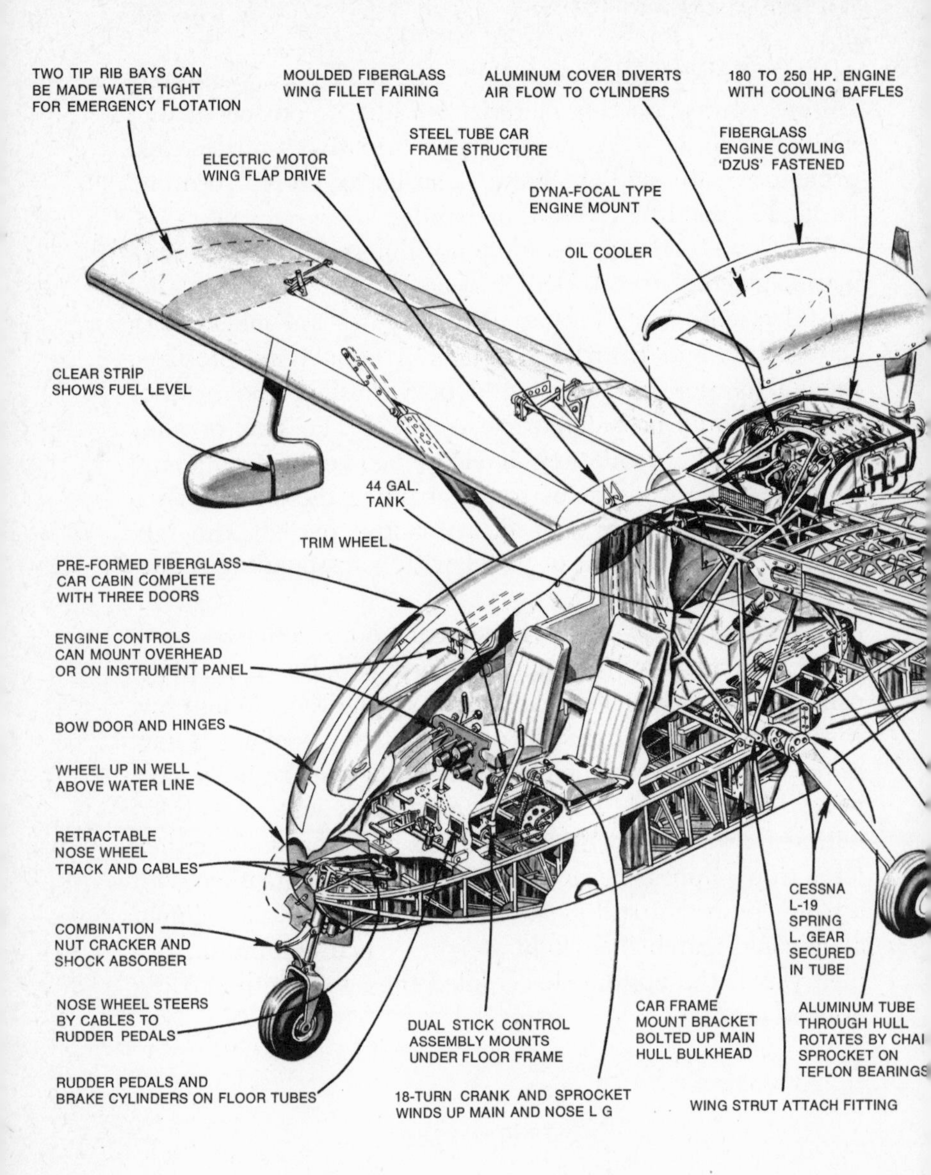
TWO TIP RIB BAYS CAN BE MADE WATER TIGHT FOR EMERGENCY FLOTATION
MOULDED FIBERGLASS WING FILLET FAIRING
ALUMINUM COVER DIVERTS AIR FLOW TO CYLINDERS
180 TO 250 HP. ENGINE WITH COOLING BAFFLES
STEEL TUBE CAR FRAME STRUCTURE
ELECTRIC MOTOR WING FLAP DRIVE
FIBERGLASS ENGINE COWLING 'DZUS' FASTENED
DYNA-FOCAL TYPE ENGINE MOUNT
OIL COOLER
CLEAR STRIP SHOWS FUEL LEVEL
44 GAL. TANK
TRIM WHEEL
PRE-FORMED FIBERGLASS CAR CABIN COMPLETE WITH THREE DOORS
ENGINE CONTROLS CAN MOUNT OVERHEAD OR ON INSTRUMENT PANEL
BOW DOOR AND HINGES
WHEEL UP IN WELL ABOVE WATER LINE
RETRACTABLE NOSE WHEEL TRACK AND CABLES
COMBINATION NUT CRACKER AND SHOCK ABSORBER
NOSE WHEEL STEERS BY CABLES TO RUDDER PEDALS
RUDDER PEDALS AND BRAKE CYLINDERS ON FLOOR TUBES
DUAL STICK CONTROL ASSEMBLY MOUNTS UNDER FLOOR FRAME
18-TURN CRANK AND SPROCKET WINDS UP MAIN AND NOSE L G
CAR FRAME MOUNT BRACKET BOLTED UP MAIN HULL BULKHEAD
CESSNA L-19 SPRING L. GEAR SECURED IN TUBE
ALUMINUM TUBE THROUGH HULL ROTATES BY CHAI SPROCKET ON TEFLON BEARINGS
WING STRUT ATTACH FITTING

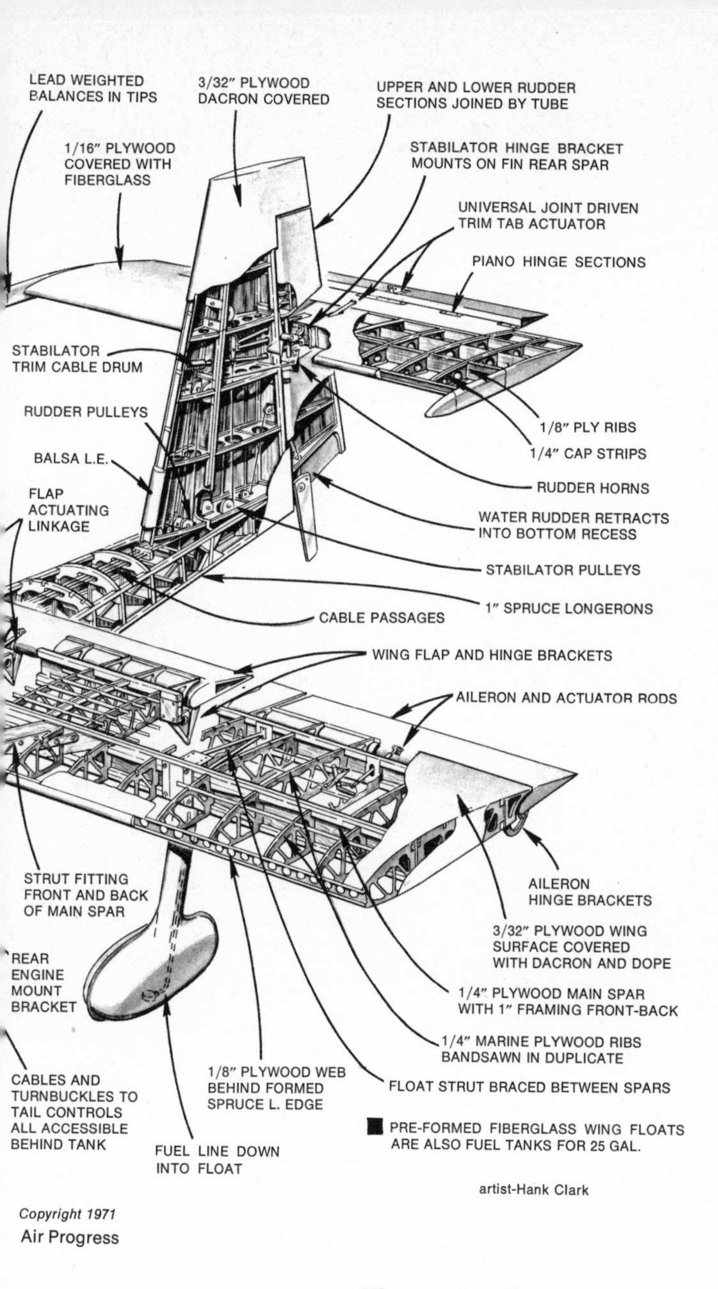

Figure 16—Spencer Air Car

hulls weigh little more than an equivalent landplane fuselage with its wheeled landing gear. To absorb rough water impacts, bottom skins run about twice as thick as hull side or fuselage skins. Bottom loads are transmitted to the sides by frequent cross frames. Some wood and fiberglass hulls have steel tube central assemblies taking the combined loads of the wing spars, the engine nacelle, and the amphibian landing gear (figure 16).

Wooden hulls have the same watertightness problems as wooden surface boats. Metal hulls are made watertight by inserting a tough fabric tape in all underwater seams before riveting. The tape is impregnated with thick bitumastic paint or zinc-chromate paste. Double rows of staggered rivets are common. After completion, metal hulls are inspected for possible leaks by filling them with water. Sometimes the leak appears on the outside a foot or more from the actual inside source, because the water has run inside the seam. When located, the leaks are sealed by squeezing a heavier, more sticky chromate or bitumastic compound into the seams. If necessary, the rivets in the faulty area are rebucked.

It surprises many that when the hull has been made watertight from water on the inside, it may still leak from the outside in when the ship is first waterborne. When such leaks occur, the area is marked afloat and repaired in the same way ashore. Once a metal hull has passed the two tests, it will remain relatively watertight for years.

FAA HULL REQUIREMENTS

As for other marine vessels, the Federal Aviation Administration requires that seaplane floats and hulls be compartmented. The two floats of a floatplane must have a combined buoyancy of 180 percent of the gross weight, and each must have four watertight compartments of approximately equal volume, so arranged that the seaplane will stay afloat when any two compartments are flooded. Below 5000 pounds gross weight, flying boat hulls must be so compartmented that they will remain afloat if any one compartment is filled. Above 5000 pounds, they must remain afloat with any two compartments filled. All bulkheads must be watertight above any possible new waterline resulting from any combination of flooding. Sometimes a section of cabin floor must also be watertight to meet this requirement. Of course, the leak inspection must also confirm the integrity of the bulkheads.

Designers rarely provided bulkheads prior to these requirements. A story that has undoubtedly grown in the telling concerns Harry Rogers, who operated flying boats out of North Beach in New York before it was named LaGuardia Airport. About 1925, Harry designed and built a new flying boat. At least the wings were modern, though the hull was a standard Curtiss Seagull. The RBX, as he named it, took off and climbed so much better than the Seagull that when taking off alone one morning to fly down the East River, Harry did not realize there was a lot of bilge water sloshing in the bottom.

He climbed steeply to fly over the Hell Gate Bridge. He succeeded, but became terrified when the ship went into an ever steeper climb as the water ran toward the tail. With the control yoke pushed full forward so hard he almost bent it, the airplane had just barely enough control to prevent a stall. The Triboro Bridge was not there in those days, and Harry hastened to get the ship down safely on the river. As he approached the water, with the bilge water now flowing toward the bow, she became so nose-heavy that a crash seemed inevitable. Now, with the yoke full back, it was a question whether she would level off in time. She did—just as he passed under the Queensborough Bridge. Harry breathed easier as he regained a safe altitude to figure out his dilemma. If he could keep his attitude level, he thought he could ease her down to the water with the throttle.

By then the lower three bridges loomed ahead and he was then flying at about bridge level. He squeezed over the Williamsburg Bridge, under the Manhattan Bridge, and over the Brooklyn Bridge, and at last had clear air ahead. By carefully juggling the throttle, and barely displacing the yoke, he finally made a fine landing off Governors Island.

21

TRENDS AND DEVELOPMENTS

As this book goes to press there is a burgeoning upsurge in seaplane orders. Edo has the highest backlog for floats in its history, with the percentage of amphibious floats steadily increasing. The Lake Aircraft Company, who manufacture the most popular little boat amphibian, have orders in hand that will bring them to the four hundred mark; 10 percent are export. The little Thurston-designed Schweizer Teal II amphibian has already won over thirty orders including many export orders, though it carries only two people. The De-Haviland turboprop Twin Otter is appearing more frequently on amphibious floats. The Down Town Flying Service is operating hourly schedules between the New York and Philadelphia waterfronts with two. The 39,000 members of the Sport Aviation Association are designing and building ever more seaplanes.

Subject to the limitations of fuel supply, there can be no doubt that water flying has a bright future, but I am too long in aviation, and too old a bird anyway, to attempt predictions. Perhaps, though, an analysis of current trends will reveal the part seaplanes may take in the coming aviation panorama. There are four dominant factors that should be defined and examined separately.

MISSIONS

Mission is a military term defining the purpose of a flight operation. It is an equally descriptive term for civil missions, which are

SPORT: Meaning fun.

UTILITY: Meaning personal, family, and convenience transportation.

BUSINESS: Meaning essential and profitable transportation within a nonaviation corporation.

COMMERCIAL: Meaning the generation of profit from the airplane itself.

AIRCRAFT SPECIFICATIONS

For each mission, the military issues specifications defining the aircraft they propose to buy. Manufacturers of civil airplanes set the specifications for the aircraft they wish to sell. Civil purchasers buy the one that best fulfills their mission, providing they can afford it. Their search for this aircraft is made in distinctive groups of airplane type or specification. Seaplanes are available under each of the following specifications.

SPORT: A basic simple airplane.

PERSONAL VFR: An airplane with more comfort and performance with simple navigation and communication equipment for private rated pilots flying under Visual Flight Rules.

PERSONAL IFR: The same, but with expensive electronic equipment for operations under Instrument Flight Rules by instrument rated pilots.

BUSINESS:	The same, but with all sophisticated equipment for high altitude and terminal airport operations flown by transport rated pilots.
COMMERCIAL:	With aircraft equipment and pilot rating to meet all the above specifications, often with larger passenger capacity, and usually flown by two pilots. Used by corporations or in short-haul scheduled transport.

RESTRICTIONS

The FAA regulatory restraints on all civil flights in the continental United States are increasing, as they must, to prevent midair collisions in areas of heavy air traffic and for noise control. These restrictions are

VISIBILITY:	The segregation of the past thirty years separating VFR flight operations from IFR operations.
ALTITUDE:	Undergoing rapid segregation for higher altitudes by equipment requirements and pilot ratings.
AREAS:	Prohibiting uncontrolled flight. Increasing rapidly.
ATC:	Air Traffic Control. Fast becoming more complex and requiring superior communications equipment and pilot ability.
NOISE:	Certain to soon bar many airplanes from many airports.

Clearly, the restrictions fall heaviest on the owners of general aviation airplanes, even though they outnumber airline and commercial types four to one, a statement that needs explanation. Out of the 135,000 or so aircraft under US Registry, and deducting the 2700 registered airliners, and the approximately 2600 Alaskan aircraft, there are about 130,000 general aviation aircraft flying in the continental US airspace. Each of these flies about 200 hours a year; those in business and airport use, more; those in personal use, somewhat less. This fleet, then, logs about 25,000,000 flying hours a year.

Airliners average about 10 flight hours a day or 3650 hours a year, of which about two-thirds is flown in daylight hours. The airline fleet logs about 6,000,000 daylight hours a year. Since the general aviation fleet flies only a little at night, it is safe to say that at any one time in daylight, there are four times as many general aviation airplanes as airliners using our precious airspace.

Federal restrictions and the cost they impose need careful analysis and prudent application if we are to preserve reasonable freedom in individual landplane flights. Seaplanes are also subject to these restrictions; however, with legal and safe flight as low as 500 feet, and the ability to land almost anywhere without air traffic control, they enjoy unique freedom.

COST

Increasing restrictions are the basic cause of skyrocketing costs. Before the restrictions escalated so severely, most intercity personal flights were completed safely on schedule with much less costly airplanes than today's. The pattern is too varied to permit conjecture on future expenses. When an owner advances from one of the aircraft specification groups to the next, he will find his total yearly expenses including depreciation, insurance, maintenance, and operating costs will generally about double. The purchaser must decide for himself how many times he can double flying expenditures. He must then be careful not to outfly the limits of the utility he has bought.

SEAPLANE MISSIONS

With only moderate assurance, we can now fit the growing seaplane activity into this trending pattern.

In the pure sport classification, which is often only a two-place airplane, and which is flown only for pleasure, there should be fast seaplane expansion. Many of the owners may go to the moderate increased expense of amphibian landing gears.

In the personal VFR class, exemplified by the fast-growing Lake Amphibians, it seems clear that their freedom from the growing restraints will win over many landplane fliers to the water.

In the personal IFR classification, which will be a relatively expensive airplane anyway, it is likely all seaplanes will be amphibians, else why equip them for IFR? Probably few of their personal owners will ever wish to outgrow this class. I believe we will soon see new designs appearing to meet this demand.

In the business class, fast amphibians with six or more seats will continue to be purchased as business machines by companies and governmental bureaus active in marine and river affairs. They will be useful wherever there are large factories or power plants at the water's edge or located out in wild country. Coastal oil-well operations will undoubtedly continue to enlarge the demand for this class.

There is also a firm, though smaller, demand for amphibians in the outright commercial field. Seaplane charter services will grow in response to increasing leisure time. The wistful hope for intercity waterfront air transport, like the

New York–Philadelphia service previously mentioned, may yet be fulfilled between the larger cities. Flight tests have shown that area navigation can bring these seaplanes with safe accuracy into New York Harbor under the controlled airline traffic above with visual breakout as low as 500 feet accurately on course.

TECHNICAL DEVELOPMENTS

Probably, recent power plant improvements will soon benefit seaplanes. Turboprops are more expensive than piston engines but should prove their worth in commercial high-performance amphibians. Recently, the installation of two Pratt and Whitney PT–6A turboprops in a Grumman Mallard greatly improved her performance with muted noise level. Waterfronts are inherently noisy places, and the volume is not greatly increased by personal seaplane operations, but for airplanes operating intimately with boats and shore homes, the hush of turboprops has a special appeal.

Q-fans get their title from "Q" for Quiet. With large bypass ratios and variable-pitch blades on the front fan, they promise a high takeoff thrust with conveniently small diameter, both features tailormade for seaplanes.

Though there has been little improvement in bottom lines in the past twenty years, further progress is assured. The underbody lines of both sailing and power yachts have undergone considerable improvement recently just after marine engineers thought they knew it all. The varied possibilities of combining water skis or hydrofoils with pneumatic floats that retract by collapsing into pockets offer the promise of lighter and faster floatplanes. The remarkable ingenuity of members of the Sport Aviation Association may be relied upon to advance this art.

A few two- and four-engine high-wing landplanes are eligible for easy redesign into flying boat amphibians. Lockheed has offered an interesting amphibian version of their turboprop military cargo plane, the C–130 Hercules. Dave Thurston made a design study for the Britten–Norman Company, manufacturers of the twin-engine Islander eight-passenger commercial landplane, for an amphibian version. It would be named the "Sealander." By simply adding a planing bottom to the fuselage, wing-tip floats, and a slightly longer landing gear, a graceful seaplane design appeared.

It was nice to have you aboard.

GLOSSARY

Amphibian A seaplane with wheels permitting it to operate also from land.

Angle of Incidence The angle at which an airfoil meets the air flow or the angle at which a wing is attached to a hull or fuselage.

Attitude The angle at which an airplane may fly or plane on the water—nose-up or nose-down.
Pitch angle.

Blipping Frequent short bursts of power.

Bottom loading The gross weight divided by the bottom area, usually in pounds per square foot.

Bridle A line in the form of a V attached at both ends.
A yoke.

Carry The residual momentum of a seaplane after the power is cut.

Center line A line through the long dimension of an object to which dimensions on each side are referred.

Center of buoyancy That point within a floating body at which the buoyancy is balanced—usually fore and aft.

Center of gravity That point within a structure at which weight is balanced in all directions or axes.

Center of resistance That point on an airplane structure where all external forces are balanced.

Centrifugal force The outward side force resulting from a curving course in flight or on water or land.

Chine The sharp break angle between the bottom and sides of a hull or float.

Configuration Engineer's term for the general structural arrangement of all the major components of an airplane.
The general shape of the aircraft.

Crabbing A sideways movement of a seaplane.

Dead rise The lateral angle from the keel to the chine.

Displacement A submerged volume. The volume below a waterline when at rest displaces a weight of water equal to the gross weight of the seaplane.

Dolly A wheeled cart especially designed to transport a seaplane for short distances.

Double curvature A sheet of thin material curved about two axes and thus not flat or rolled.

Eye A spliced loop at the end of a line.

Fair An adjective applying to a curved line or surface which has no breaks or irregularities. A verb when such a surface is made to be fair.

Flake To allow a line to fall free into a pile so that it will pay out without snarling.

Float A buoyancy chamber attached to an airplane to support it and plane on the water.
A floating dock.

Floatplane A seaplane in the configuration of a landplane with several floats attached to permit water operations.

Fluke The extended hook or horn of an anchor.

Flying boat A seaplane carrying passengers and cargo within a hull to which wings and tail are attached.

Free board The height above water of the lowest large hull opening that could fill with water.

Ground cushion The additional lift occurring when an airplane is close to the ground (or water).

Heave The up-and-down movement of a hull but without pitch.

Hump The speed at which a seaplane makes the transition from the displacement condition to the planing phase.

Hydro-airplane An airplane capable of landing and takeoff from the water.
A seaplane.

Hydrofoil An underwater lifting surface in the shape of a small wing.

Hydroplane A surface boat that planes on the water only.

IFR—Instrument Flight Rules. A flight requiring a Flight Clearance and the use of Flight Instruments made by a pilot with an Instrument Rating.

Keel effect The tendency of a keel to resist sideways movement on the water or to resist turns from a straight course.

Leeway The drift away from a desired course caused by the wind.

Mach number A measurement of flight speed. Mach 1 is the speed of sound, which varies with altitude and temperature.

Pay out To extend the free length of a line.

Pennant The permanent short line on a mooring buoy.

Pitch angle The angle at which an airplane may fly or plane on the water—nose-up or nose-down.
Attitude.

Porpoising A rhythmic pitching motion nose-up and nose-down.

Power loading The gross weight divided by the total power, usually in pounds per horsepower.

Prada A waterfront park in Latin-speaking countries.

Pylon A streamlined supporting post.

Race rotation The twisting flow within the prop slipstream.

Ramp A sloping runway for launching seaplanes from land.

Range A sighted line on fixed objects.

Rotation The termination of a takeoff where an airplane is pitched upward to climb.

RPM Revolutions per minute, as of an engine or propeller.

Sailing Using the wind to assist in taxiing along a desired course.

Scope The length of an anchor or tow line.

Seawings Short airfoil-shaped extensions from a hull at the waterline providing lateral stability on the water.
Sponsons.

Skipping An up-and-down motion while taxiing—more in heave than pitch.

Span The major lateral dimension of an aircraft from wing tip to wing tip.

Sponson An extension on the waterline of a flying boat hull.
A sea wing.

Step The sharp break in a hull or float bottom slightly aft of the center of gravity.

Sublimate The direct transition of ice to vapor without passing through the liquid state.

Taxiing Moving an airplane over land or water surface.

Thrust line The extended line through the propeller shaft or jet tail pipe.

Torque The twisting force on an airplane from the reaction of power to the propeller(s).

Trim Refers to the stabilizer setting at which an airplane flies hands off, or to the residual nose or tail heaviness if it is out of trim.

Unport The point at which a submerged planing surface climbs to the surface.

VFR—Visual Flight Rules. A flight made without instruments with location determined by visual observation of the ground.

Waterline The line at which the water laps the side of a hull—either at rest (displacement) or when moving through the water.

Water loop A violent swerve to the side during fast taxiing, similar to a ground loop on land.

Water ski A water planing surface in the general shape of a snow ski.

Waves See pages 83-94 for definitions of all components.

Weather-cocking The tendency of a seaplane to point into the wind.

Wing loading The gross weight divided by the wing area, usually in pounds per square foot.

Yaw Turning force or rotation about the vertical axis through the center of gravity.

Yoke A line in the form of a V attached at both ends.
A bridle.

Index

(Chapter headings appear in *Italics*. Page numbers referring to illustrations and diagrams appear in *Italics*.)